Groovy Sounds
A Journey Through 1960s British Rock N Roll
Vol. 1
Trivia Quiz Book

Christian Scott

ISBN: 9798877524910

DEDICATION

For the Rebels and the Dreamers,

This book is dedicated to those who embraced the power of music to transcend time and space. To the rebels who danced to the beats of change and the dreamers who found solace in the melodies that echoed through the ages. Your passion and spirit have inspired these pages, and it's to you that this journey belongs. May the rhythms of these words resonate with the beats of your heart.

To the Icons who Shaped the Sounds,

In honor of the trailblazers who etched their stories into the vinyl of history, whose voices still echo in the corridors of time. From the Beatles to the Stones, from Pink Floyd to the Who, this dedication is a humble tribute to the legends who dared to dream and, in doing so, created the soundtrack of our lives.

For the Love of Rock 'n' Roll,

Introduction:

Welcome to "Groovy Sounds: A Journey Through 1960s British Rock N Roll"! The 1960s was an era that reverberated with the electrifying sounds of British rock 'n' roll, giving birth to timeless classics, iconic bands, and a cultural revolution that would leave an indelible mark on music history. This trivia book is your ticket to relive the magic, discover hidden gems, and test your knowledge about the dynamic and diverse landscape of British rock music during this transformative decade.

In the following pages, we'll take you on a nostalgic ride through the birth of Freakbeat, the psychedelic explosion, the rise of the British Invasion bands and the emergence of legendary acts that defined the era. From Liverpool, Manchester and Birmingham to London, the sounds of the '60s British rock scene were as diverse as the nation itself. Whether you're a die-hard fan or a curious explorer of musical history, prepare to delve into the trivia, anecdotes, and stories that shaped the unforgettable melodies of this remarkable period.

The queries in this book revolve around rock bands that originated in the 1960s. Some questions delve into the later years of these bands/artists and their impact on the genre.

Every effort has been made by the author and publisher of this book to provide accurate information on the subject of this book. Even though the information in this book has been carefully checked and researched, the author and publisher disclaim any responsibility for errors in the book.

So, turn up the volume, get ready to test your knowledge, and join us as we explore the rich tapestry of 1960s British rock 'n' roll!

CONTENTS

ACKNOWLEDGMENTS

Gratitude in Stereo
Completing this journey through the annals of musical history has been an
exhilarating experience, and I extend my deepest gratitude to the individuals and
entities who made this endeavor a reality:

The Maestros of Influence:
To the pioneers of rock 'n' roll, whose groundbreaking work laid the foundation for
this exploration. Your impact on music and culture is immeasurable, and this work is
a humble homage to your enduring legacy.

The Librarians of Sound:
A heartfelt thank you to the libraries, archives, and institutions that provided access to
rare recordings, photographs, and historical documents. Your dedication to preserving
the musical past is a gift to present and future generations.

The Collaborative Ensemble:
I express my appreciation to the scholars, experts, and fellow enthusiasts who
generously shared their insights, anecdotes, and passion for the subject matter. Your
collaborative spirit has added depth and nuance to these pages.

The Supporters and Champions:
To my friends, family, and mentors – your unwavering support, encouragement, and
belief in this project have been invaluable. Your enthusiasm has fueled my own, and I
am grateful for the shared excitement for the world of rock 'n' roll.

The Sonic Architects:
Deep gratitude to the producers, engineers, and technicians whose sonic
craftsmanship shaped the music we celebrate in these pages. Your meticulous work
behind the mixing console has left an indelible mark on the soundscape of history.

The Readers and Explorers:
Last but certainly not least, to the readers and explorers who embark on this musical
journey – thank you for choosing to be a part of this symphony. May the tales within
these pages resonate with you as much as the music itself.

As the final chord of this project rings out, I am humbled by the collective effort that
brought it to fruition. This book is a celebration of shared passion, and I am grateful
for each note contributed to its composition.

The Action (Answers Page 7)

1. What was the original name of the 1960s British rock band "The Action"?
   a) The Rolling Stones
   b) The Yardbirds
   c) The Boys
   d) The In Crowd

2. In which city did The Action originate and establish themselves as a prominent part of the British rock scene?
   a) Liverpool
   b) London
   c) Manchester
   d) Birmingham

3. Which member of The Action later became a key figure in the influential band, Thunderclap Newman?
   a) Reggie King
   b) Alan King
   c) Pete Townshend
   d) Roger Powell

4. What was The Action's debut single, released in 1965, that gained them recognition in the British music scene?
   a) "Something to Say"
   b) "I'll Keep on Holding On"
   c) "Land of a Thousand Dances"
   d) "Shadows and Reflections"

5. The Action's musical style evolved from R&B to a more psychedelic sound. Which album marked this transition?
   a) "Rolled Gold"
   b) "Action Packed"
   c) "The Ultimate Action"
   d) "Brain"

6. Which famous record producer worked with The Action on their unreleased album "Rolled Gold" in 1967?
   a) George Martin
   b) Phil Spector
   c) Jimmy Miller
   d) Joe Meek

The Action (Answers Page 7)

7. What led to The Action disbanding in the late 1960s?
    a) Creative differences
    b) Financial troubles
    c) Legal issues
    d) Personal commitments

Andromeda (Answers Page 7)

8. What was the debut album of the 1960s British rock band
    Andromeda?
    a) "Wings of Love"
    b) "Andromeda Rising"
    c) "Cannock"
    d) "Turns to Dust"

9. Who was the lead guitarist of Andromeda during their active
    years in the 1960s?
    a) John Cann
    b) Dave Lewis
    c) Jack McCulloch
    d) Mick Hawksworth

10. Which British rock festival did Andromeda perform in 1969?
    a) Isle of Wight Festival
    b) Glastonbury Festival
    c) Reading Festival
    d) Woodstock Festival

11. What label released Andromeda's single "Go Your Way"?
    a) EMI Records
    b) Decca Records
    c) RCA Victor
    d) Harvest Records

12. Which member of Andromeda was responsible for vocals
    and flute?
    a) John Cann
    b) Mick Hawksworth
    c) Jack McCulloch
    d) Ian McLane

Andromeda (Answers Page 7)

13. In 1969, Andromeda released an album titled:
    a) "Echoes of Love and Destruction"
    b) "Return to Sanity"
    c) "Galaxy Voyage"
    d) "Starlight Serenade"

14. Which of the following songs is NOT a track from
    Andromeda's album "Turns to Dust"?
    a) "Timothy's Sunday"
    b) "Sleep Like a Child"
    c) "Garden of Happiness"
    d) "Too Old"

The Animals (Answers Page 7)

15. What was the original name of the 1960s British rock band
    "The Animals"?
    a) The Yardbirds
    b) The Kinks
    c) The Animals
    d) The Rolling Stones

16. Which hit single released by The Animals in 1964 became an
    international sensation and topped the charts in the United
    States?
    a) "House of the Rising Sun"
    b) "We Gotta Get Out of This Place"
    c) "Don't Let Me Be Misunderstood"
    d) "It's My Life"

17. What instrument did Eric Burdon, the lead singer of The
    Animals, play in the band?
    a) Guitar
    b) Keyboards
    c) Bass
    d) Harmonica

The Animals (Answers Page 7)

18. The Animals' rendition of "The House of the Rising Sun" is a traditional folk song, but who is credited for the arrangement in their version?
a) Bob Dylan
b) Lead Belly
c) Woody Guthrie
d) Pete Seeger

19. In 1966, The Animals released an album that featured the hit single "Don't Bring Me Down." What was the name of this album?
a) "The Animals"
b) "Animal Tracks"
c) "Animalism"
d) "Eric Is Here"

20. Which member of The Animals later formed the band War and had a successful career in the 1970s?
a) Hilton Valentine
b) Chas Chandler
c) Eric Burdon
d) Alan Price

21. What is the title of The Animals' 1965 album that includes the hit songs "We Gotta Get Out of This Place" and "It's My Life"?
a) "Animal Tracks"
b) "Animalisms"
c) "The Animals on Tour"
d) "Animalization"

22. The Animals had a hit with the song "Don't Let Me Be Misunderstood." Who wrote this song?
a) Eric Burdon
b) Nina Simone
c) Billy Joel
d) Randy Newman

The Animals (Answers Page 7)

23. Which city served as the hometown for The Animals during their formative years?
    a) Liverpool
    b) Manchester
    c) Birmingham
    d) Newcastle

24. What was the final studio album released by The Animals before their initial disbandment in 1969?
    a) "Animalization"
    b) "The Twain Shall Meet"
    c) "Every One of Us"
    d) "Love Is"

25. The original guitarist of The Animals, who played on their early hits, was replaced by another guitarist. What was the name of the original guitarist?
    a) Alan Price
    b) Chas Chandler
    c) Dave Rowberry
    d) Hilton Valentine

26. In 1994, The Animals were inducted into the Rock and Roll Hall of Fame. Which city is home to the Rock and Roll Hall of Fame?
    a) Los Angeles
    b) Nashville
    c) Cleveland
    d) Memphis

The Action (Answers)

1. c) The Boys
2. b) London
3. b) Alan King
4. b) "I'll Keep on Holding On"
5. d) "Brain"
6. a) George Martin
7. b) Financial troubles

Andromeda (Answers)

8. b) "Andromeda Rising"
9. a) John Cann
10. a) Isle of Wight Festival
11. a) EMI Records
12. d) Ian McLane
13. b) "Return to Sanity"
14. c) "Garden of Happiness"

The Animals (Answers)

15. c) The Animals
16. a) "House of the Rising Sun"
17. d) Harmonica
18. b) Lead Belly
19. c) "Animalism"
20. c) Eric Burdon
21. d) "Animalization"
22. b) Nina Simone
23. d) Newcastle
24. c) "Every One of Us"
25. d) Hilton Valentine
26. c) Cleveland

Atomic Rooster (Answers Page 14)

27. Who was the founding member and keyboardist of the 1960s
British rock band Atomic Rooster?
a) Vincent Crane
b) Carl Palmer
c) John Du Cann
d) Nick Graham

28. Which Atomic Rooster album, released in 1970, features the
hit single "Tomorrow Night"?
a) "Death Walks Behind You"
b) "In Hearing of Atomic Rooster"
c) "Atomic Rooster"
d) "Nice 'n' Greasy"

29. What instrument did John Du Cann primarily play in Atomic
Rooster?
a) Guitar
b) Bass
c) Drums
d) Vocals

30. Which drummer joined Atomic Rooster in 1970,
contributing to the album "Death Walks Behind You"?
a) Carl Palmer
b) Simon Kirke
c) Paul Hammond
d) Mick Underwood

31. What was the last studio album released by Atomic Rooster
in the 1960s?
a) "Atomic Rooster"
b) "Death Walks Behind You"
c) "In Hearing of Atomic Rooster"
d) "Nice 'n' Greasy"

32. Which song from the album "Death Walks Behind You" is
considered one of Atomic Rooster's signature tracks?
a) "Breakthrough"
b) "Tomorrow Night"
c) "Devil's Answer"
d) "The Price"

Atomic Rooster (Answers Page 14)

33. After Vincent Crane's departure, which musician became the lead vocalist and keyboardist for Atomic Rooster?
    a) Adrian Gurvitz
    b) Pete French
    c) Bernie Tormé
    d) Chris Farlowe

The Attack (Answers Page 14)

34. What was the original name of the 1960s British rock band "The Attack" before they changed it to The Attack?
    a) The Thunderbolts
    b) The Invaders
    c) The Renegades
    d) The Prowlers

35. The Attack gained popularity for their energetic live performances in the London music scene. Which famous venue did they often play at?
    a) The Cavern Club
    b) The Marquee Club
    c) The Whisky a Go Go
    d) The Fillmore East

36. Who was the lead vocalist of The Attack, known for his powerful and distinctive voice?
    a) Richard Shirman
    b) Davy O'List
    c) John Du Cann
    d) Gerry Henderson

37. In 1967, The Attack released a single that became one of their most recognized songs. What is the title of this single?
    a) "Neville Thumbcatch"
    b) "Created by Clive"
    c) "Hi Ho Silver Lining"
    d) "Magic in the Air"

The Attack (Answers Page 14)

38. Which member of The Attack later joined The Nice, a
    progressive rock band formed by Keith Emerson?
    a) Gerry Henderson
    b) Davy O'List
    c) Richard Shirman
    d) Alan White

39. The Attack's music is often associated with the mod and
    psychedelic rock movements. What was the title of their only
    studio album, released in 1968?
    a) "Hi Ho Silver Lining"
    b) "Magic in the Air"
    c) "About Time"
    d) "Now You Know"

40. What influential music producer worked with The Attack on
    their single "Hi Ho Silver Lining" in 1967?
    a) George Martin
    b) Joe Meek
    c) Mickie Most
    d) Chris Blackwell

41. The Attack's original lineup underwent changes over the
    years. Which member went on to become a member of
    Atomic Rooster in the early 1970s?
    a) Gerry Henderson
    b) Davy O'List
    c) John Du Cann
    d) Richard Shirman

The Beatles (Answers Page 14)

42. Who was the youngest member of The Beatles?
    a) John Lennon
    b) Paul McCartney
    c) George Harrison
    d) Ringo Starr

43. Which Beatles album is often considered the band's masterpiece and one of the greatest albums of all time?
    a) "Help!"
    b) "Rubber Soul"
    c) "The White Album"
    d) "Abbey Road"

44. What was the title of The Beatles' first feature film released in 1964?
    a) "Let It Be"
    b) "A Hard Day's Night"
    c) "Help!"
    d) "Yellow Submarine"

45. Which Beatles song features a sitar played by George Harrison and was influenced by Indian classical music?
    a) "Twist and Shout"
    b) "Norwegian Wood (This Bird Has Flown)"
    c) "Lucy in the Sky with Diamonds"
    d) "Yesterday"

46. What was the last studio album recorded by The Beatles before their breakup in 1970?
    a) "Let It Be"
    b) "Magical Mystery Tour"
    c) "The White Album"
    d) "Abbey Road"

47. Who wrote the majority of The Beatles' songs along with John Lennon?
    a) Paul McCartney
    b) George Harrison
    c) Ringo Starr
    d) Brian Epstein

The Beatles (Answers Page 14)

48. What is the name of the animated film featuring The Beatles
    and released in 1968?
    a) "A Hard Day's Night"
    b) "Help!"
    c) "Yellow Submarine"
    d) "Let It Be"

49. Which Beatles album includes the tracks "Eleanor Rigby"
    and "Yellow Submarine"?
    a) "Revolver"
    b) "Sgt. Pepper's Lonely Hearts Club Band"
    c) "Rubber Soul"
    d) "The Beatles (The White Album)"

50. Who was the original drummer of The Beatles before being
    replaced by Ringo Starr?
    a) Pete Best
    b) Stuart Sutcliffe
    c) Billy Preston
    d) Klaus Voormann

51. Which Beatles song features a reversed guitar solo and was
    part of the "Revolver" album?
    a) "A Day in the Life"
    b) "Tomorrow Never Knows"
    c) "While My Guitar Gently Weeps"
    d) "I Am the Walrus"

52. In which year did The Beatles make their famous debut on
    The Ed Sullivan Show in the United States?
    a) 1962
    b) 1964
    c) 1966
    d) 1968

53. What was the title of The Beatles' 1st single released in 1962?
    a) "Love Me Do"
    b) "Twist and Shout"
    c) "Can't Buy Me Love"
    d) "I Want to Hold Your Hand"

The Beatles (Answers Page 14)

54. Which member of The Beatles was known as "the quiet one"?
    a) John Lennon
    b) Paul McCartney
    c) George Harrison
    d) Ringo Starr

55. What was the final studio album released by The Beatles before their breakup?
    a) "Let It Be"
    b) "Abbey Road"
    c) "The White Album"
    d) "Revolver"

56. Which Beatles song features a groundbreaking music video and was released in 1967?
    a) "A Hard Day's Night"
    b) "Hey Jude"
    c) "I Am the Walrus"
    d) "Strawberry Fields Forever"

Atomic Rooster (Answers)

27. a) Vincent Crane
28. b) "In Hearing of Atomic Rooster"
29. a) Guitar
30. c) Paul Hammond
31. a) "Atomic Rooster"
32. c) "Devil's Answer"
33. a) Adrian Gurvitz

The Attack (Answers)

34. a) The Thunderbolts
35. b) The Marquee Club
36. a) Richard Shirman
37. b) "Created by Clive"
38. b) Davy O'List
39. c) "About Time"
40. c) Mickie Most
41. c) John Du Cann

The Beatles (Answers)

42. c) George Harrison
43. d) "Abbey Road"
44. b) "A Hard Day's Night"
45. b) "Norwegian Wood (This Bird Has Flown)"
46. a) "Let It Be"
47. a) Paul McCartney
48. c) "Yellow Submarine"
49. a) "Revolver"
50. a) Pete Best
51. b) "Tomorrow Never Knows"
52. b) 1964
53. a) "Love Me Do"
54. c) George Harrison
55. b) "Abbey Road"
56. d) "Strawberry Fields Forever

The Jeff Beck Group (Answers Page 20)

57. Who was the lead guitarist of the 1960s British rock band
    The Jeff Beck Group?
    a) Jimmy Page
    b) Jeff Beck
    c) Eric Clapton
    d) Ritchie Blackmore

58. Which renowned vocalist fronted The Jeff Beck Group and
    later went on to form the band Faces with Rod Stewart?
    a) Paul Rodgers
    b) Robert Plant
    c) Roger Daltrey
    d) Rod Stewart

59. The Jeff Beck Group released their debut album in 1968.
    What is the title of this album?
    a) "Truth"
    b) "Blow by Blow"
    c) "Rough and Ready"
    d) "Beck-Ola"

60. Who was the bassist for The Jeff Beck Group, known for his
    work with other legendary rock bands like The Faces and
    Small Faces?
    a) John Entwistle
    b) Jack Bruce
    c) Ron Wood
    d) Tim Bogert

61. Which Jeff Beck Group album, released in 1969, featured the
    hit song "Let Me Love You" with Rod Stewart on vocals?
    a) "Beck-Ola"
    b) "Rough and Ready"
    c) "Truth"
    d) "Jeff Beck Group"

The Jeff Beck Group (Answers Page 20)

62. What was the name of the drummer who played with The Jeff Beck Group and later became a member of Led Zeppelin?
    a) Mitch Mitchell
    b) John Bonham
    c) Ginger Baker
    d) Carmine Appice

63. Which Jeff Beck Group album showcased a more soulful and bluesy sound, released in 1971 after Rod Stewart and Ron Wood had left the band?
    a) "Beck-Ola"
    b) "Blow by Blow"
    c) "Rough and Ready"
    d) "Jeff Beck Group"

64. Before joining The Jeff Beck Group, Rod Stewart and Ron Wood were part of a band with a distinctive name. What was the name of this band?
    a) The Small Faces
    b) The Faces
    c) The Yardbirds
    d) The Animals

65. Which song from The Jeff Beck Group's debut album "Truth" is known for its bluesy guitar riff and has been covered by various artists?
    a) "Beck's Bolero"
    b) "Rock My Plimsoul"
    c) "Shapes of Things"
    d) "Morning Dew"

66. The Jeff Beck Group underwent multiple lineup changes. Which keyboardist was a member of the band during their early years and played on the album "Truth"?
    a) Rick Wakeman
    b) John Paul Jones
    c) Nicky Hopkins
    d) Keith Emerson

Maggie Bell (Answers Page 20)

67. Before joining Stone the Crows, Maggie Bell was a member
of which Scottish blues-rock band?
a) Free
b) Nazareth
c) The Sensational Alex Harvey Band
d) Frankie Miller's Full House

68. What's the title of Maggie Bell's debut album, from 1974?
a) "Queen of the Night"
b) "Suicide Sal"
c) "Blood on the Tracks"
d) "Hard Woman"

69. In the 1960s, Maggie Bell was the lead vocalist for which
blues-rock band that tragically lost its guitarist, Les Harvey,
during a performance?
a) Stone the Crows
b) Fleetwood Mac
c) Cream
d) The Yardbirds

70. Maggie Bell collaborated with which ex-Free guitarist on the
album "Suicide Sal"?
a) Mick Ralphs
b) Paul Kossoff
c) Andy Fraser
d) Paul Rodgers

71. Which American rock band did Maggie Bell join for a brief
period in the late 1970s?
a) The Rolling Stones
b) Jefferson Airplane
c) Little Feat
d) The Allman Brothers Band

72. Maggie Bell is often regarded as one of the finest female rock
vocalists. What is her vocal range known for?
a) Soprano
b) Alto
c) Mezzo-soprano
d) Tenor

Maggie Bell (Answers Page 20)

73. In 2016, Maggie Bell released a collaborative album with which fellow Scottish singer-songwriter?
a) Lulu
b) Susan Boyle
c) Annie Lennox
d) Eddi Reader

Cliff Bennett And The Rebel Rousers
(Answers Page 20)

74. Who was the lead vocalist and frontman of Cliff Bennett and the Rebel Rousers?
a) Cliff Richard
b) Cliff Bennett
c) Eric Burdon
d) Cliff Edwards

75. Cliff Bennett and the Rebel Rousers' version of "Got to Get You into My Life" was written by which iconic songwriting duo?
a) Lennon and McCartney
b) Jagger and Richards
c) Bacharach and David
d) Leiber and Stoller

76. In 1966, the band released a successful single titled:
a) "A Hard Day's Night"
b) "One Way Love"
c) "Paint It, Black"
d) "Good Vibrations"

77. Cliff Bennett and the Rebel Rousers were associated with which British music label?
a) EMI
b) Decca
c) Parlophone
d) Pye

Cliff Bennett And The Rebel Rousers
(Answers Page 20)

78. The Rebel Rousers backed which American rock and roll legend during some of their performances?
a) Chuck Berry
b) Little Richard
c) Jerry Lee Lewis
d) Fats Domino

79. What was the title of Cliff Bennett and the Rebel Rousers' debut album, released in 1964?
a) "Shout"
b) "Drivin' You Wild"
c) "One Way Love"
d) "At Abbey Road"

80. Which Beatles song, later covered by Cliff Bennett and the Rebel Rousers, features a brass section arranged by George Martin?
a) "Hey Jude"
b) "A Hard Day's Night"
c) "Can't Buy Me Love"
d) "Twist and Shout"

The Jeff Beck Group (Answers)

57. b) Jeff Beck
58. d) Rod Stewart
59. a) "Truth"
60. c) Ron Wood
61. d) "Jeff Beck Group"
62. b) John Bonham
63. c) "Rough and Ready"
64. a) The Small Faces
65. a) "Beck's Bolero"
66. c) Nicky Hopkins

Maggie Bell (Answers)

67. c) The Sensational Alex Harvey Band
68. a) "Queen of the Night"
69. a) Stone the Crows
70. b) Paul Kossoff
71. c) Little Feat
72. c) Mezzo-soprano
73. d) Eddi Reader

Cliff Bennett And The Rebel Rousers (Answers)

74. b) Cliff Bennett
75. a) Lennon and McCartney
76. b) "One Way Love"
77. a) EMI
78. b) Little Richard
79. a) "Shout"
80. c) "Can't Buy Me Love"

The Big Three (Answers Page 27)

81. Who were the original members of The Big Three?
    a) Brian Epstein, George Martin, and Pete Best
    b) Johnny Hutchinson, Adrian Barber, and Johnny Gustafson
    c) John Lennon, Paul McCartney, and George Harrison
    d) Mick Jagger, Keith Richards, and Brian Jones

82. The Big Three were closely associated with which city's music scene during the 1960s?
    a) Manchester
    b) Liverpool
    c) London
    d) Birmingham

83. Which of the following songs is a notable cover recorded by The Big Three?
    a) "Twist and Shout"
    b) "I Wanna Hold Your Hand"
    c) "I'm Down"
    d) "Some Other Guy"

84. The Big Three disbanded in 1966. After the breakup, Johnny Hutchison joined a band with which famous guitarist?
    a) Eric Clapton
    b) Jimmy Page
    c) Jeff Beck
    d) Pete Townshend

85. The Big Three played regularly at which legendary Liverpool venue during their prime?
    a) The Cavern Club
    b) The Casbah Coffee Club
    c) The Jacaranda
    d) The Grapes

86. Which member of The Big Three later became a successful record producer?
    a) Johnny Hutchinson
    b) Adrian Barber
    c) Johnny Gustafson

d) None of the above
The Birds (Answers Page 27)

87. What was the original name of the 1960s British rock band "The Birds" before they changed it to The Birds?
    a) The Thunderbirds
    b) The Byrds
    c) The Ravens
    d) The Crawdaddies

88. Which well-known musician, who later achieved fame with The Jeff Beck Group and Faces, was a founding member of The Birds?
    a) Rod Stewart
    b) Ronnie Wood
    c) Jeff Beck
    d) Jimmy Page

89. The Birds were part of the R&B and blues scene in London. What instrument did Ron Wood play in the band?
    a) Guitar
    b) Bass
    c) Drums
    d) Keyboard

90. In 1965, The Birds released a single that gained popularity in the mod scene. What is the title of this single?
    a) "Eight Miles High"
    b) "Turn! Turn! Turn!"
    c) "Leaving Here"
    d) "Mr. Tambourine Man"

91. The Birds' music was influenced by American R&B, and they were known for covering songs by which legendary blues artist?
    a) Muddy Waters
    b) B.B. King
    c) Howlin' Wolf
    d) Robert Johnson

The Birds (Answers Page 27)

92. What was the reason behind The Birds' decision to change
their name to The Birds Birds in 1966?
a) Legal issues with another band named The Birds
b) Creative differences among band members
c) A suggestion from their record label
d) Superstition regarding the original name

93. The Birds were known for their energetic live performances.
Which London club, famous for hosting emerging bands, did
they frequently play at?
a) The Cavern Club
b) The Marquee Club
c) The Roundhouse
d) The 100 Club

Black Cat Bones (Answers Page 27)

94. Who was the founding member and lead guitarist of Black
Cat Bones?
a) Paul Kossoff
b) Paul Rodgers
c) Mick Jagger
d) Paul "Shorty" Williams

95. Black Cat Bones is often associated with which music genre?
a) Psychedelic rock
b) Progressive rock
c) Blues rock
d) Folk rock

96. Before forming Free, Paul Kossoff and Simon Kirke of
Black Cat Bones joined forces with which vocalist and bassist
to create the early lineup of Free?
a) Roger Waters
b) Andy Fraser
c) John Paul Jones
d) Jack Bruce

Black Cat Bones (Answers Page 27)

97. Black Cat Bones released an album in 1969 titled:
    a) "Barbed Wire Sandwich"
    b) "Black Cat Blues"
    c) "Cat Scratch Fever"
    d) "Bones of Contention"

98. Which Black Cat Bones song, featuring Paul Kossoff's guitar work, is often cited as one of their notable tracks?
    a) "Feelin' Good"
    b) "Crossroads"
    c) "Deserted Cities of the Heart"
    d) "Boogie for George"

Black Sabbath (Answers Page 27)

99. Who was the lead guitarist and primary songwriter for Black Sabbath?
    a) Tony Iommi
    b) Ozzy Osbourne
    c) Geezer Butler
    d) Bill Ward

100. Which Black Sabbath album is often considered the birth of heavy metal and was released in 1970?
    a) "Paranoid"
    b) "Master of Reality"
    c) "Black Sabbath"
    d) "Vol. 4"

101. What was the original name of Black Sabbath before they changed it to "Black Sabbath"?
    a) Earth
    b) Brimstone
    c) Coven
    d) Pentagram

Black Sabbath (Answers Page 27)

102. Which Black Sabbath song features the ominous opening riff and the tolling church bells?
a) "Iron Man"
b) "War Pigs"
c) "N.I.B."
d) "Black Sabbath"

103. Who replaced Ozzy Osbourne as the lead vocalist of Black Sabbath in 1979?
a) Ronnie James Dio
b) Ian Gillan
c) Glenn Hughes
d) Rob Halford

104. Which Black Sabbath album marked the debut of Ronnie James Dio as the lead vocalist?
a) "Sabotage"
b) "Heaven and Hell"
c) "Technical Ecstasy"
d) "Mob Rules"

105. What was Black Sabbaths 3rd studio album released in 1971?
a) "Paranoid"
b) "Master of Reality"
c) "Black Sabbath Vol. 4"
d) "Sabbath Bloody Sabbath"

106. Which member of Black Sabbath is known for playing the bass guitar and contributing to songwriting?
a) Ozzy Osbourne
b) Tony Iommi
c) Geezer Butler
d) Bill Ward

107. In 1969, Black Sabbath released their self-titled debut album. What was its original title before being changed?
a) "Heavy Metal Mass"
b) "Witches' Sabbath"
c) "Black Sunday"

d) "The End of the Beginning"

Black Sabbath (Answers Page 27)

108. Which Black Sabbath album features the song "Iron Man" and was released in 1970?
a) "Paranoid"
b) "Master of Reality"
c) "Black Sabbath Vol. 4"
d) "Sabbath Bloody Sabbath"

The Big Three (Answers)

81. b) Johnny Hutchinson, Adrian Barber, and Johnny Gustafson
82. b) Liverpool
83. d) "Some Other Guy"
84. c) Jeff Beck
85. a) The Cavern Club
86. b) Adrian Barber

The Birds (Answers)

87. a) The Thunderbirds
88. b) Ronnie Wood
89. a) Guitar
90. c) "Leaving Here"
91. c) Howlin' Wolf
92. a) Legal issues with another band named The Birds
93. b) The Marquee Club

Black Cat Bones (Answers)

94. a) Paul Kossoff
95. c) Blues rock
96. b) Andy Fraser
97. a) "Barbed Wire Sandwich"
98. a) "Feelin' Good"

Black Sabbath (Answers)

99. a) Tony Iommi
100. a) "Paranoid"
101. a) Earth
102. d) "Black Sabbath"
103. a) Ronnie James Dio
104. b) "Heaven and Hell"
105. b) "Master of Reality"
106. c) Geezer Butler
107. c) "Black Sunday"
108. a) "Paranoid"

Blind Faith (Answers Page 34)

109. Who was the lead guitarist of Blind Faith, known for his
     work with Cream?
     a) Eric Clapton
     b) Jimmy Page
     c) Jeff Beck
     d) Pete Townshend

110. Blind Faith's self-titled debut album was released in which
     year?
     a) 1968
     b) 1969
     c) 1970
     d) 1971

111. Who was the lead vocalist of Blind Faith, also known for his
     role in Traffic and later as a solo artist?
     a) Steve Winwood
     b) Roger Daltrey
     c) Robert Plant
     d) Ian Gillan

112. Which legendary drummer, previously with Cream, played in
     Blind Faith?
     a) Ginger Baker
     b) Mitch Mitchell
     c) Keith Moon
     d) John Bonham

113. What was the hit single from Blind Faith's debut album that
     reached the top of the charts in the UK?
     a) "Can't Find My Way Home"
     b) "Presence of the Lord"
     c) "Had to Cry Today"
     d) "Sea of Joy"

114. Blind Faith's cover art for their debut album features a
     controversial photograph by which photographer?
     a) Annie Leibovitz
     b) Linda McCartney
     c) Robert Mapplethorpe
     d) Bob Seidemann

Blind Faith (Answers Page 34)

115. Before the formation of Blind Faith, Eric Clapton and
Ginger Baker were members of which rock band?
a) The Yardbirds
b) The Animals
c) Cream
d) The Rolling Stones

116. What was the title of Blind Faith's only studio album?
a) "Blind Faith"
b) "Presence of the Lord"
c) "Can't Find My Way Home"
d) "Sea of Joy"

117. Which member of Blind Faith later joined the supergroup
Derek and the Dominos with Eric Clapton?
a) Steve Winwood
b) Ginger Baker
c) Ric Grech
d) Jim Capaldi

118. Blind Faith disbanded after only one album and tour. What
year did they officially disband?
a) 1969
b) 1970
c) 1971
d) 1972

David Bowie (Answers Page 34)

119. What was David Bowie's birth name?
a) David Robert Jones
b) Duncan Jones
c) Brian Jones
d) Ziggy Stardust

David Bowie (Answers Page 34)

120. Which iconic alter ego did David Bowie adopt during the early 1970s, associated with the album "The Rise and Fall of Ziggy Stardust and the Spiders from Mars"?
a) The Thin White Duke
b) Major Tom
c) Ziggy Stardust
d) Aladdin Sane

121. What was David Bowie's first major hit single released in 1969?
a) "Space Oddity"
b) "Starman"
c) "Heroes"
d) "Changes":

122. Which album marked David Bowie's shift to a more soul and funk-oriented sound and includes the hit single "Fame"?
a) "The Rise and Fall of Ziggy Stardust and the Spiders from Mars"
b) "Young Americans"
c) "Hunky Dory"
d) "Station to Station"

123. David Bowie's character in the film "The Man Who Fell to Earth" is named:
a) Ziggy Stardust
b) Major Tom
c) Thomas Jerome Newton
d) The Thin White Duke

124. Which album by David Bowie features the song "Life on Mars?" and was released in 1971?
a) "Low"
b) "Hunky Dory"
c) "Aladdin Sane"
d) "Diamond Dogs"

David Bowie (Answers Page 34)

125. In 1969, David Bowie collaborated with which legendary
     guitarist on the album "Space Oddity"?
     a) Eric Clapton
     b) Jeff Beck
     c) Jimmy Page
     d) Mick Ronson

126. Which song by David Bowie, released in 1977, features a
     distinctive guitar riff and is considered one of his signature
     tracks?
     a) "Heroes"
     b) "Rebel Rebel"
     c) "Suffragette City"
     d) "Jean Genie"

127. David Bowie's final studio album, released in 2016, is titled:
     a) "Blackstar"
     b) "The Next Day"
     c) "Reality"
     d) "Heathen"

Budgie (Answers Page 34)

128. In what year was the rock band Budgie formed?
     a) 1967
     b) 1969
     c) 1971
     d) 1973

129. Who was the founding member and lead vocalist/bassist of
     Budgie?
     a) Tony Bourge
     b) Burke Shelley
     c) Ray Phillips
     d) Steve Williams

Budgie (Answers Page 34)

130. Which Budgie album, released in 1971, is often considered a classic of the heavy metal genre and features the iconic track "Breadfan"?
a) "Squawk"
b) "In for the Kill"
c) "Budgie"
d) "Never Turn Your Back on a Friend"

131. Budgie's sound is often associated with a blend of hard rock and which other musical genre?
a) Jazz
b) Blues
c) Folk
d) Progressive rock

132. Budgie's drummer Ray Phillips was replaced by this drummer in 1974. Who was he?
a) Simon Phillips
b) Pete Boot
c) Steve Williams
d) Robert "Congo" Jones

Caravan (Answers Page 34)

133. Who was the founder and original keyboardist of Caravan?
a) Richard Coughlan
b) Pye Hastings
c) David Sinclair
d) Geoff Richardson

134. Which city is Caravan associated with, often considered a part of the Canterbury scene of progressive rock?
a) London
b) Manchester
c) Canterbury
d) Liverpool

Caravan (Answers Page 34)

135. Caravan's debut album, released in 1968, is titled:
     a) "In the Land of Grey and Pink"
     b) "Caravan"
     c) "If I Could Do It All Over Again, I'd Do It All Over You"
     d) "Waterloo Lily"

136. Which member of Caravan is known for playing the flute
     and contributed to the band's early sound?
     a) Pye Hastings
     b) Richard Coughlan
     c) David Sinclair
     d) Jimmy Hastings

137. Caravan's album "In the Land of Grey and Pink" features
     the notable track:
     a) "Golf Girl"
     b) "Nine Feet Underground"
     c) "Winter Wine"
     d) "Love to Love You (And Tonight Pigs Will Fly)"

138. Which Caravan album, released in 1973, is known for its jazz
     fusion elements and features the track "The Dabsong
     Conshirtoe"?
     a) "Cunning Stunts"
     b) "For Girls Who Grow Plump in the Night"
     c) "Waterloo Lily"
     d) "Caravan and the New Symphonia"

Blind Faith (Answers)

109. a) Eric Clapton
110. c) 1970
111. a) Steve Winwood
112. a) Ginger Baker
113. a) "Can't Find My Way Home"
114. d) Bob Seidemann
115. c) Cream
116. a) "Blind Faith"
117. c) Ric Grech
118. b) 1970

David Bowie (Answers)

119. a) David Robert Jones
120. c) Ziggy Stardust
121. a) "Space Oddity"
122. b) "Young Americans"
123. c) Thomas Jerome Newton
124. b) "Hunky Dory"
125. d) Mick Ronson
126. b) "Rebel Rebel"
127. a) "Blackstar"

Budgie (Answers)

128. b) 1969
129. b) Burke Shelley
130. a) "Squawk"
131. c) Folk
132. c) Steve Williams

Caravan (Answers)

133. c) David Sinclair
134. c) Canterbury
135. b) "Caravan"
136. d) Jimmy Hastings
137. b) "Nine Feet Underground"
138. a) "Cunning Stunts"

Eric Clapton (Answers Page 41)

139. Which iconic British rock band did Eric Clapton join in 1963, marking the beginning of his fame?
a) The Rolling Stones
b) The Who
c) Cream
d) The Yardbirds

140. What is the title of Eric Clapton's debut solo album released in 1970?
a) "Slowhand"
b) "461 Ocean Boulevard"
c) "Layla and Other Assorted Love Songs"
d) "Eric Clapton"

141. In 1966, Eric Clapton formed the supergroup Cream with which bassist and drummer?
a) Jack Bruce and Ginger Baker
b) John Paul Jones and John Bonham
c) John Entwistle and Keith Moon
d) Paul McCartney and Ringo Starr

142. Which Eric Clapton song, released in 1974, became a hit and is a tribute to his son Conor?
a) "Layla"
b) "Tears in Heaven"
c) "Crossroads"
d) "Wonderful Tonight"

143. What is the nickname often associated with Eric Clapton due to his smooth guitar playing style?
a) Slowhand
b) The Guitar Wizard
c) The Blues Maestro
d) The Stratocaster King

Eric Clapton (Answers Page 41)

144. Which classic rock song by Derek and the Dominos, led by
Eric Clapton, features the famous guitar riff and was released
in 1970?
a) "Layla"
b) "Sunshine of Your Love"
c) "White Room"
d) "Cocaine"

145. Eric Clapton's unplugged performance of "Tears in Heaven"
won which major music award in 1993?
a) Grammy Award
b) Brit Award
c) MTV Music Award
d) American Music Award

146. Which blues standard, covered by Eric Clapton, became a
chart-topping single in 1970?
a) "Crossroads"
b) "Before You Accuse Me"
c) "Key to the Highway"
d) "Sweet Home Chicago"

147. In 1968, Eric Clapton participated in a collaborative project
known as the "Super Session" with which other renowned
guitarist?
a) Jimi Hendrix
b) Jeff Beck
c) Jimmy Page
d) Duane Allman

The Dave Clark Five (Answers Page 41)

148. Who was the leader and drummer of the Dave Clark Five?
a) Mike Smith
b) Lenny Davidson
c) Dave Clark
d) Rick Huxley

The Dave Clark Five (Answers Page 41)

149. What was the debut single of the Dave Clark Five that
   became a hit in both the UK and the US?
   a) "Bits and Pieces"
   b) "Glad All Over"
   c) "Catch Us If You Can"
   d) "Do You Love Me"

150. Which member of the Dave Clark Five played the keyboards
   and sang lead vocals on many of their songs?
   a) Lenny Davidson
   b) Mike Smith
   c) Dave Clark
   d) Rick Huxley

151. What was the title of the Dave Clark Five's only film,
   released in 1965?
   a) "Glad All Over Again"
   b) "Having a Wild Weekend"
   c) "Bits and Pieces"
   d) "Do You Love Me"

152. Which Dave Clark Five hit single features the famous
   opening drum riff and was released in 1964?
   a) "Glad All Over"
   b) "Because"
   c) "Catch Us If You Can"
   d) "Bits and Pieces"

153. What was the name of the Dave Clark Five's bassist who
   passed away in 2013?
   a) Denis Payton
   b) Mike Smith
   c) Lenny Davidson
   d) Rick Huxley

154. In which year did the Dave Clark Five disband?
   a) 1965
   b) 1968
   c) 1970
   d) 1972

The Dave Clark Five (Answers Page 41)

155. What was a nickname for the fans of the Dave Clark Five?
    a) Beatlemaniacs
    b) Clarkettes
    c) Davesters
    d) Five-ers

156. The Dave Clark Five's song "Over and Over" was later
    covered by which American rock and roll artist?
    a) Chuck Berry
    b) Little Richard
    c) Buddy Holly
    d) Elvis Presley

157. What was the last top-ten hit single for the Dave Clark Five,
    released in 1969?
    a) "Glad All Over"
    b) "Red Balloon"
    c) "You Got What It Takes"
    d) "Catch Us If You Can"

158. Which member of the Dave Clark Five was known for his
    guitar playing and backing vocals?
    a) Mike Smith
    b) Lenny Davidson
    c) Rick Huxley
    d) Dave Clark

159. The Dave Clark Five's album "American Tour" was
    recorded during their tour in which year?
    a) 1963
    b) 1965
    c) 1967
    d) 1969

160. What was the title of the Dave Clark Five's first studio
    album released in 1964?
    a) "Glad All Over"
    b) "A Session with the Dave Clark Five"
    c) "American Tour"
    d) "Five by Five"

The Dave Clark Five (Answers Page 41)

161. Which of the following songs by the Dave Clark Five was
     nominated for a Grammy Award for Best Rock and Roll
     Recording in 1965?
     a) "Glad All Over"
     b) "Bits and Pieces"
     c) "Because"
     d) "Do You Love Me"

Joe Cocker (Answers Page 41)

162. Joe Cocker gained widespread recognition for his distinctive
     cover of a Beatles song that became a Woodstock anthem.
     Which song is it?
     a) "Come Together"
     b) "Let It Be"
     c) "Something"
     d) "With a Little Help from My Friends"

163. In 1969, Joe Cocker performed at the iconic Woodstock
     Festival. What was the name of his backing band at that
     historic event?
     a) The Band
     b) The Grease Band
     c) The Wrecking Crew
     d) The Silver Bullet Band

164. Which Joe Cocker album, released in 1969, features the hit
     singles "Feelin' Alright" and "Delta Lady"?
     a) "Mad Dogs & Englishmen"
     b) "With a Little Help from My Friends"
     c) "Joe Cocker!"
     d) "Sheffield Steel"

165. What is the title of the song from the movie "9½ Weeks"
     that was covered by Joe Cocker and became a hit in 1986?
     a) "Unchain My Heart"
     b) "You Are So Beautiful"
     c) "Up Where We Belong"
     d) "With a Little Help from My Friends"

Joe Cocker (Answers Page 41)

166. Joe Cocker won a Grammy Award for Best Pop
Performance by a Duo or Group with Vocal for a duet with
which female artist?
a) Tina Turner
b) Whitney Houston
c) Jennifer Warnes
d) Stevie Nicks

167. Which Joe Cocker song, originally by Randy Newman,
became a chart-topping hit for him in 1970 and earned him a
Grammy Award?
a) "Feelin' Alright"
b) "You Can Leave Your Hat On"
c) "Up Where We Belong"
d) "Delta Lady"

168. Joe Cocker's live album and film, released in 1970, captured
his performances during a U.S. tour. What is the title of this
album and film?
a) "Mad Dogs & Englishmen"
b) "Cocker Happy"
c) "Woodstock Revisited"
d) "Live at the Fillmore East"

169. Joe Cocker's rendition of "With a Little Help from My
Friends" became the theme song for a popular television
series. Which series used his version as its theme?
a) "Friends"
b) "The Wonder Years"
c) "Cheers"
d) "The Sopranos"

Eric Clapton (Answers)

139. d) The Yardbirds
140. d) "Eric Clapton"
141. a) Jack Bruce and Ginger Baker
142. b) "Tears in Heaven"
143. a) Slowhand
144. a) "Layla"
145. a) Grammy Award
146. c) "Key to the Highway"
147. b) Jeff Beck

The Dave Clark Five (Answers)

148. c) Dave Clark
149. b) "Glad All Over"
150. b) Mike Smith
151. b) "Having a Wild Weekend"
152. a) "Glad All Over"
153. d) Rick Huxley
154. c) 1970
155. b) Clarkettes
156. d) Elvis Presley
157. b) "Red Balloon"
158. b) Lenny Davidson
159. c) 1967
160. b) "A Session with the Dave Clark Five"
161. d) "Do You Love Me"

Joe Cocker (Answers)

162. d) "With a Little Help from My Friends"
163. b) The Grease Band
164. c) "Joe Cocker!"
165. a) "Unchain My Heart"
166. c) Jennifer Warnes
167. b) "You Can Leave Your Hat On"
168. a) "Mad Dogs & Englishmen"
169. b) "The Wonder Years"

Colonel Bagshot (Answers Page 48)

170. Who was the lead vocalist of Colonel Bagshot?
    a) Ken Hensley
    b) Nigel Luby
    c) Brian Farrell
    d) Rod Argent

171. Colonel Bagshot gained recognition for their song "Six Day War." What was the theme of this song?
    a) Anti-war protest
    b) Love and romance
    c) Political satire
    d) Space exploration

172. The band's name, Colonel Bagshot, is a reference to a character in which classic literary work?
    a) Moby-Dick
    b) War and Peace
    c) The Catcher in the Rye
    d) Alice's Adventures in Wonderland

173. Colonel Bagshot's music is often categorized under which genre?
    a) Psychedelic rock
    b) Progressive rock
    c) Blues rock
    d) Folk rock

174. The song "Six Day War" gained renewed popularity in the 21st century when it was featured in the soundtrack of which film?
    a) Forrest Gump
    b) Apocalypse Now
    c) The Big Lebowski
    d) Reservoir Dogs

The Crazy World Of Arthur Brown (Answers Page 48)

175. What was the signature hit song for The Crazy World of
Arthur Brown released in 1968?
a) "White Room"
b) "Sunshine of Your Love"
c) "Fire"
d) "Purple Haze"

176. What distinctive element did Arthur Brown often
incorporate into his stage performances?
a) Pyrotechnics and fire
b) Puppetry and marionettes
c) Mime and silent acting
d) Acrobatics and gymnastics

177. The Crazy World of Arthur Brown's debut album, released
in 1968, is titled:
a) "Fire and Water"
b) "The Crazy World of Arthur Brown"
c) "In Rock"
d) "Axis: Bold as Love"

178. Which instrument did Vincent Crane play in The Crazy
World of Arthur Brown?
a) Guitar
b) Organ
c) Bass
d) Drums

179. In 1968, The Crazy World of Arthur Brown's theatrical style
influenced the creation of which famous rock band's stage
presence?
a) Led Zeppelin
b) The Rolling Stones
c) Pink Floyd
d) Alice Cooper

The Crazy World Of Arthur Brown (Answers Page 48)

180. What was the follow-up album to "The Crazy World of Arthur Brown," released in 1969?
a) "Strangelands"
b) "Journey"
c) "Galactic Zoo Dossier"
d) "Inferno"

181. What was the name of Arthur Brown's headdress, a trademark of his stage persona?
a) The Fiery Crown
b) The Cosmic Helmet
c) The Enigmatic Turban
d) The God of Hellfire Hat

Cream (Answers Page 48)

182. Who was the lead guitarist of Cream?
a) Eric Clapton
b) Jack Bruce
c) Ginger Baker
d) Jimmy Page

183. What was Cream's debut album released in 1966?
a) "Disraeli Gears"
b) "Wheels of Fire"
c) "Fresh Cream"
d) "Goodbye"

184. Which Cream song features a famous bass solo by Jack Bruce and was released in 1967?
a) "White Room"
b) "Badge"
c) "Sunshine of Your Love"
d) "Crossroads"

Cream (Answers Page 48)

185. Cream's "Sunshine of Your Love" is known for its distinctive:
    a) Drum solo
    b) Bass line
    c) Guitar riff
    d) Keyboard solo

186. What was the title of Cream's double album released in 1968, which includes live and studio recordings?
    a) "Goodbye"
    b) "Disraeli Gears"
    c) "Wheels of Fire"
    d) "Live Cream"

187. Which member of Cream was known for his exceptional drumming skills and was a jazz-influenced percussionist?
    a) Eric Clapton
    b) Jack Bruce
    c) Ginger Baker
    d) Mitch Mitchell

188. Cream disbanded in 1968 after the release of their fourth studio album. What is the title of that album?
    a) "Goodbye"
    b) "Disraeli Gears"
    c) "Wheels of Fire"
    d) "Fresh Cream"

189. Which Cream song is a cover of a Robert Johnson blues classic and was featured on their debut album?
    a) "Strange Brew"
    b) "Crossroads"
    c) "I Feel Free"
    d) "Politician"

Cream (Answers Page 48)

190. In 1993, Cream reunited for a series of concerts at which
     iconic venue?
     a) Royal Albert Hall
     b) Madison Square Garden
     c) Hollywood Bowl
     d) Fillmore East

Creation (Answers Page 48)

191. Who was the lead vocalist and guitarist of the 1960s British
     rock band Creation?
     a) Eric Clapton
     b) Kenny Pickett
     c) Pete Townshend
     d) Jeff Beck

192. Which Creation hit single, released in 1966, is known for its
     garage rock sound and catchy chorus?
     a) "Painter Man"
     b) "Making Time"
     c) "If I Stay Too Long"
     d) "Cool Jerk"

193. Creation's debut single "Making Time" was featured in
     which iconic 1960s film?
     a) "Easy Rider"
     b) "Blow-Up"
     c) "A Hard Day's Night"
     d) "The Graduate"

194. Which English record producer and songwriter was a
     founding member of Creation and co-wrote their hit "Painter
     Man"?
     a) Tony Visconti
     b) Joe Meek
     c) Mickie Most
     d) Shel Talmy

Creation (Answers Page 48)

195. Creation's only studio album, released in 1967, is titled:
   a) "We Are Paintermen"
   b) "The Creation Collection"
   c) "Making Time"
   d) "Painter Man"

196. Which famous guitarist, known for his work with The Yardbirds and Led Zeppelin, briefly played with Creation?
   a) Jeff Beck
   b) Eric Clapton
   c) Jimmy Page
   d) Ritchie Blackmore

197. Creation's music style is often associated with which genre that emerged in the 1960s?
   a) Psychedelic rock
   b) Progressive rock
   c) Folk rock
   d) Glam rock

Colonel Bagshot (Answers)

170. b) Nigel Luby
171. a) Anti-war protest
172. d) Alice's Adventures in Wonderland
173. a) Psychedelic rock
174. c) The Big Lebowski

The Crazy World Of Arthur Brown (Answers)

175. c) "Fire"
176. a) Pyrotechnics and fire
177. b) "The Crazy World of Arthur Brown"
178. b) Organ
179. d) Alice Cooper
180. c) "Galactic Zoo Dossier"
181. a) The Fiery Crown

Cream (Answers)

182. a) Eric Clapton
183. c) "Fresh Cream"
184. b) "Badge"
185. c) Guitar riff
186. c) "Wheels of Fire"
187. c) Ginger Baker
188. a) "Goodbye"
189. b) "Crossroads"
190. a) Royal Albert Hall

Creation (Answers)

191. b) Kenny Pickett
192. a) "Painter Man"
193. b) "Blow-Up"
194. a) Tony Visconti
195. a) "We Are Paintermen"
196. c) Jimmy Page
197. a) Psychedelic rock

Lee Curtis And The All Stars (Answers Page 55)

198. Lee Curtis and the All-Stars originated from which English city's music scene?
    a) Liverpool
    b) Manchester
    c) London
    d) Birmingham

199. What was the band's first single, released in 1964?
    a) "Little Children"
    b) "Funny How Love Can Be"
    c) "Shakin' All Over"
    d) "Let's Stomp"

200. Which influential Liverpool music manager handled Lee Curtis and the All-Stars?
    a) Brian Epstein
    b) Larry Parnes
    c) Joe Meek
    d) Allan Williams

201. Lee Curtis briefly left the band in 1964, and during his absence, who filled in as the lead vocalist?
    a) Cilla Black
    b) Pete Best
    c) Billy J. Kramer
    d) Rory Storm

202. Lee Curtis and the All-Stars released a single that was a cover of a song by which American rock and roll artist?
    a) Chuck Berry
    b) Little Richard
    c) Buddy Holly
    d) Fats Domino

203. Lee Curtis later became a member of which popular British band known for its Merseybeat sound?
    a) The Searchers
    b) Gerry and the Pacemakers
    c) The Hollies
    d) The Merseybeats

Spencer Davis Group (Answers Page 55)

204. What was the name of the lead vocalist and primary
songwriter for the Spencer Davis Group?
a) Steve Marriott
b) Steve Winwood
c) Eric Burdon
d) Graham Nash

205. The Spencer Davis Group had a major hit single in 1966
that topped the charts in both the UK and the US. What was
the title of this song?
a) "I'm a Man"
b) "Gimme Some Lovin'"
c) "Keep on Running"
d) "Somebody Help Me"

206. Which instrument did Spencer Davis himself play in the
group?
a) Guitar
b) Organ
c) Bass
d) Drums

207. In addition to Steve Winwood, which member of the
Spencer Davis Group later had a successful solo career,
including hits like "Higher Love"?
a) Muff Winwood
b) Pete York
c) Chris Wood
d) Jim Capaldi

208. The Spencer Davis Group's hit single "I'm a Man" featured
a distinctive instrument in its introduction. What was that
instrument?
a) Harmonica
b) Saxophone
c) Hammond organ
d) Tambourine

Spencer Davis Group (Answers Page 55)

209. What was the title of the Spencer Davis Group's debut
    studio album, released in 1965?
    a) "Autumn '66"
    b) "I'm a Man"
    c) "Gimme Some Lovin'"
    d) "Their First LP"

210. The Spencer Davis Group collaborated with which famous
    record producer on several of their early hits, including
    "Keep on Running" and "Gimme Some Lovin'"?
    a) George Martin
    b) Phil Spector
    c) Jimmy Miller
    d) Joe Meek

211. What was the nationality of the Spencer Davis Group's
    drummer, Pete York?
    a) British
    b) American
    c) Canadian
    d) Australian

212. The Spencer Davis Group's song "Keep on Running" (1965)
    was originally written and recorded by which American
    artist?
    a) Chuck Berry
    b) Ray Charles
    c) Otis Redding
    d) Jackie Edwards

213. After Steve Winwood left the Spencer Davis Group in 1967,
    the band continued with a new lead vocalist. Who replaced
    Winwood?
    a) Dave Mason
    b) Jim Capaldi
    c) Chris Wood
    d) Eddie Hardin

Deep Purple (Answers Page 55)

214. Who was the founding member and keyboardist of Deep
Purple?
a) Ritchie Blackmore
b) Ian Gillan
c) Jon Lord
d) Roger Glover

215. Which Deep Purple album, released in 1972, includes the
iconic track "Smoke on the Water"?
a) "Deep Purple in Rock"
b) "Machine Head"
c) "Fireball"
d) "Who Do We Think We Are"

216. Who was the lead vocalist of Deep Purple during their
classic lineup and the recording of "Smoke on the Water"?
a) Ian Gillan
b) David Coverdale
c) Rod Evans
d) Glenn Hughes

217. Deep Purple's classic lineup is often referred to as "Mark II"
and includes all of the following members except:
a) Ritchie Blackmore
b) Ian Gillan
c) Jon Lord
d) Roger Waters

218. Which Deep Purple album, released in 1969, is considered a
landmark in the development of hard rock and heavy metal?
a) "In Rock"
b) "Shades of Deep Purple"
c) "The Book of Taliesyn"
d) "Fireball"

Deep Purple (Answers Page 55)

219. What is the title of the instrumental track by Deep Purple that became one of their signature tunes and is featured on the album "Machine Head"?
a) "Highway Star"
b) "Smoke on the Water"
c) "Lazy"
d) "Space Truckin'"

220. Deep Purple's "Made in Japan" is a live album recorded during which tour?
a) "Machine Head" Tour
b) "Perfect Strangers" Tour
c) "Fireball" Tour
d) "Burn" Tour

221. Which guitarist was known for his distinctive playing style and co-founded Deep Purple with Jon Lord?
a) Steve Morse
b) Ritchie Blackmore
c) Joe Satriani
d) Tommy Bolin

222. Deep Purple's album "Burn," released in 1974, marked the debut of which vocalist?
a) Ian Gillan
b) David Coverdale
c) Rod Evans
d) Glenn Hughes

The Dennisons (Answers Page 55)

223. Who was the lead vocalist of The Dennisons?
a) Clive Hornby
b) Phil Coulter
c) Eddie Amoo
d) John Lacey
Correct Answer:

The Dennisons (Answers Page 55)

224. The Dennisons were associated with which major British city's music scene?
a) London
b) Manchester
c) Liverpool
d) Birmingham
Correct Answer:

225. What was the title of The Dennisons' debut single, released in 1963?
a) "Walkin' the Dog"
b) "Be My Girl"
c) "Nobody Like My Baby"
d) "Denise, Denise"
Correct Answer:

226. The Dennisons were contemporaries of which more famous Liverpool band and shared the same manager, Brian Epstein?
a) The Rolling Stones
b) The Kinks
c) The Beatles
d) The Who
Correct Answer:

227. In addition to their musical career, some members of The Dennisons later found success in which other field?
a) Acting
b) Politics
c) Journalism
d) Culinary arts
Correct Answer:

Lee Curtis And The All Stars (Answers)

198. a) Liverpool
199. d) "Let's Stomp"
200. a) Brian Epstein
201. b) Pete Best
202. b) Little Richard
203. d) The Merseybeats

Spencer Davis Group (Answers)

204. b) Steve Winwood
205. b) "Gimme Some Lovin'"
206. a) Guitar
207. d) Jim Capaldi
208. c) Hammond organ
209. d) "Their First LP"
210. d) Joe Meek
211. b) American
212. d) Jackie Edwards
213. a) Dave Mason

Deep Purple (Answers)

214. c) Jon Lord
215. b) "Machine Head"
216. a) Ian Gillan
217. d) Roger Waters
218. a) "In Rock"
219. c) "Lazy"
220. a) "Machine Head" Tour
221. b) Ritchie Blackmore
222. b) David Coverdale

The Dennisons (Answers)

223. a) Clive Hornby
224. c) Liverpool
225. b) "Be My Girl"
226. c) The Beatles
227. a) Acting

The Deviants (Answers Page 61)

228. Who was the founding member and frontman of The Deviants?
a) Mick Farren
b) Paul Rudolph
c) Duncan Sanderson
d) Russell Hunter

229. The Deviants' music is often associated with which subgenre of rock?
a) Progressive rock
b) Psychedelic rock
c) Blues rock
d) Folk rock

230. In addition to their music, The Deviants were known for their involvement in which counterculture movement?
a) Dadaism
b) Situationism
c) Fluxus
d) Dandyism

231. The Deviants released their debut album in 1967. What was the title of this album?
a) "Ptooff!"
b) "Disposable"
c) "Deviate and Derange"
d) "Psychedelic Noise Freakout"

232. Mick Farren, the lead singer of The Deviants, was also known for his work as a:
a) Visual artist
b) Science fiction author
c) Political activist
d) Chef

Donovan (Answers Page 61)

233. What is Donovan's full birth name?
   a) Donovan Leitch
   b) Donovan Phillips Leitch
   c) Donovan St. Patrick Leitch
   d) Donovan Michael Leitch

234. Donovan's hit song "Mellow Yellow" is known for featuring which distinctive instrument?
   a) Sitar
   b) Flute
   c) Harmonica
   d) Mellotron

235. In 1965, Donovan released an album titled "Sunshine Superman." What genre is prominently associated with this?
   a) Folk
   b) Psychedelic rock
   c) Blues
   d) Country

236. Which of Donovan's songs became an anthem for the hippie movement and is considered one of his signature tracks?
   a) "Hurdy Gurdy Man"
   b) "Catch the Wind"
   c) "Atlantis"
   d) "Sunshine Superman"

237. Donovan's debut single, released in 1965, is titled:
   a) "Mellow Yellow"
   b) "Sunshine Superman"
   c) "Catch the Wind"
   d) "Hurdy Gurdy Man"

238. Which famous American musician and songwriter collaborated with Donovan on the song "Season of the Witch"?
   a) Bob Dylan
   b) Jim Morrison
   c) Brian Wilson

d) John Lennon

Donovan (Answers Page 61)

239. Donovan's album "The Hurdy Gurdy Man" features a collaboration with which member of The Beatles?
    a) Paul McCartney
    b) John Lennon
    c) George Harrison
    d) Ringo Starr

240. Which instrument did Donovan often incorporate into his music, contributing to his unique sound?
    a) Banjo
    b) Dulcimer
    c) Bagpipes
    d) Didgeridoo

241. Donovan's song "Jennifer Juniper" is inspired by a famous actress. Who is Jennifer Juniper in real life?
    a) Mia Farrow
    b) Brigitte Bardot
    c) Jane Fonda
    d) Julie Christie

The End (Answers Page 61)

242. Who was the founding member and lead singer of The End?
    a) Terry Taylor
    b) Roger Groom
    c) Colin Griffin
    d) David Brown

243. The End is associated with which genre of rock music?
    a) Psychedelic rock
    b) Progressive rock
    c) Blues rock
    d) Garage rock

244. What was the title of The End's debut single, from 1965?
    a) "Shades of Orange"
    b) "Please Kill Me"
    c) "Introspection"

d) "Cardboard Watch"
The End (Answers Page 61)

245. The End released their only studio album in 1969. What was the title of this album?
a) "Introspection"
b) "The End"
c) "Shades of Orange"
d) "Retrospection"

246. The End's sound is often characterized by the use of:
a) Sitar
b) Violin
c) Organ
d) Bagpipes

The Equals (Answers Page 61)

247. The Equals were a 1960s British rock band known for their hit "Baby, Come Back." Who was the lead singer of the band?
a) Denny Laine
b) Eddy Grant
c) Eric Burdon
d) Georgie Fame

248. The Equals' breakthrough single, "Baby, Come Back," was released in 1968. What was the band's original name before they became The Equals?
a) The Equals
b) The Sensational Equals
c) The Equals Five
d) The Equals Trio

249. In addition to Eddy Grant, which member of The Equals was known for his distinctive dance moves and contributed to the band's energetic stage presence?
a) Derv Gordon
b) Lincoln Gordon
c) Pat Lloyd
d) John Hall

The Equals (Answers Page 61)

250. The Equals' song "Police on My Back" gained renewed popularity when it was covered by which punk rock band in the 1980s?
a) The Clash
b) Sex Pistols
c) Ramones
d) The Damned

251. The Equals' music was characterized by a fusion of different genres. What style of music was a significant influence on their sound?
a) Reggae
b) Jazz
c) Country
d) Blues

252. What was the title of The Equals' debut album released in 1967?
a) "Baby, Come Back"
b) "Equals Strike Again"
c) "First Among Equals"
d) "Unequalled Equals"

253. The Equals had a string of hits in the late 1960s. Which one of the following songs was NOT a chart-topping hit for the band?
a) "Baby, Come Back"
b) "Black Skin Blue Eyed Boys"
c) "Viva Bobby Joe"
d) "I Get So Excited"

The Deviants (Answers)

228. a) Mick Farren
229. b) Psychedelic rock
230. b) Situationism
231. a) "Ptooff!"
232. c) Political activist

Donovan (Answers)

233. b) Donovan Phillips Leitch
234. a) Sitar
235. b) Psychedelic rock
236. c) "Atlantis"
237. c) "Catch the Wind"
238. a) Bob Dylan
239. c) George Harrison
240. b) Dulcimer
241. d) Julie Christie

The End (Answers)

242. c) Colin Griffin
243. a) Psychedelic rock
244. d) "Cardboard Watch"
245. a) "Introspection"
246. c) Organ

The Equals (Answers)

247. b) Eddy Grant
248. c) The Equals Five
249. b) Lincoln Gordon
250. a) The Clash
251. a) Reggae
252. d) "Unequalled Equals"
253. d) "I Get So Excited"

The Escorts (Answers Page 67)

254. Who was the lead vocalist of The Escorts?
    a) Mick Jagger
    b) Terry Sylvester
    c) Mike Peters
    d) Roy Phillips

255. The Escorts gained popularity in the 1960s with their hit single:
    a) "A Whiter Shade of Pale"
    b) "Let It Be"
    c) "All Over Now"
    d) "Dizzy Miss Lizzy"

256. In addition to Terry Sylvester, which future member of The Hollies was part of The Escorts?
    a) Allan Clarke
    b) Graham Nash
    c) Tony Hicks
    d) Bernie Calvert

257. The Escorts' music is often associated with which genre?
    a) Psychedelic rock
    b) Blues rock
    c) Folk rock
    d) Merseybeat

258. What was the title of The Escorts' debut album, from 1964?
    a) "All Over Now"
    b) "From the Beginning"
    c) "Make Me Belong to You"
    d) "The Escorts"

The Eyes (Answers Page 67)

259. What was the original name of the 1960s British rock band "The Eyes" before they changed it to The Eyes?
    a) The Spectacles
    b) The Watchers
    c) The Gazers

d) The Observers

The Eyes (Answers Page 67)

260. The Eyes gained recognition as part of the mod and psychedelic rock scene in London. What iconic venue did they often perform at in the mid-1960s?
a) The Cavern Club
b) The Roundhouse
c) The Marquee Club
d) The 100 Club

261. Who was the lead vocalist and principal songwriter for The Eyes?
a) Jeff Beck
b) Paul McCartney
c) Ken Whaley
d) Chris Lovegrove

262. The Eyes released a single in 1966 that gained attention for its rebellious lyrics. What is the title of this song?
a) "When the Night Falls"
b) "I'm Rowed Out"
c) "Good Day Sunshine"
d) "See That Girl"

263. Which member of The Eyes later joined the influential British rock band The Pretty Things in the late 1960s?
a) Phil May
b) Dick Taylor
c) Wally Waller
d) Brian Pendleton

264. The Eyes' music evolved from R&B to a more psychedelic sound. What was the title of their only studio album, released in 1966?
a) "The Eyes"
b) "In Sight"
c) "My Degeneration"
d) "Scopophilia"

The Eyes (Answers Page 67)

265. What was the reason behind The Eyes disbanding in the late
     1960s?
     a) Creative differences
     b) Lack of commercial success
     c) Managerial disputes
     d) Personal commitments

Fairport Convention (Answers Page 67)

266. Who was the founding member and lead guitarist of
     Fairport Convention in the 1960s?
     a) Richard Thompson
     b) Sandy Denny
     c) Simon Nicol
     d) Dave Pegg

267. Fairport Convention's critically acclaimed album "Liege &
     Lief" (1969) is often regarded as pioneering which music
     genre?
     a) Psychedelic Rock
     b) Progressive Rock
     c) Folk Rock
     d) Blues Rock

268. What traditional English folk song, featured on "Liege &
     Lief," became one of Fairport Convention's signature tunes?
     a) "Who Knows Where the Time Goes?"
     b) "Tam Lin"
     c) "Matty Groves"
     d) "Crazy Man Michael"

269. Which member of Fairport Convention wrote the iconic
     song "Who Knows Where the Time Goes?"?
     a) Richard Thompson
     b) Dave Swarbrick
     c) Sandy Denny
     d) Martin Lamble

Fairport Convention (Answers Page 67)

270. Fairport Convention organized the annual music festival known as:
a) Woodstock
b) Isle of Wight Festival
c) Cropredy Festival
d) Glastonbury Festival

271. What tragic event occurred in 1969 that deeply affected Fairport Convention, leading to a significant change in their lineup?
a) Plane crash
b) Studio fire
c) Riot at a concert
d) Band members' illness

Georgie Fame (& The Blue Flames)
(Answers Page 67)

272. Who was the lead singer and frontman of the 1960s British rock band Georgie Fame and the Blue Flames?
a) Georgie Harrison
b) Georgie Foster
c) Georgie Fame
d) Georgie Turner

273. Which instrument did Georgie Fame primarily play in addition to providing vocals for the band?
a) Guitar
b) Saxophone
c) Organ
d) Trumpet

274. Georgie Fame and the Blue Flames achieved commercial success with the hit single "Yeh, Yeh" in 1964. Who wrote this song?
a) Georgie Fame
b) Paul McCartney
c) Van Morrison
d) Burt Bacharach

Georgie Fame (& The Blue Flames)
(Answers Page 67)

275. In 1966, Georgie Fame and the Blue Flames released an album featuring the popular track "Get Away." What is the title of this album?
a) "Sound Venture"
b) "Rhythm and Blues at the Flamingo"
c) "Sweet Things"
d) "Two Faces of Fame"

276. Which music genre was Georgie Fame and the Blue Flames primarily associated with during the 1960s?
a) Psychedelic Rock
b) Jazz
c) Folk Rock
d) Rhythm and Blues

277. Which iconic music venue in London was closely associated with Georgie Fame and the Blue Flames, serving as a hub for the British jazz and rhythm and blues scene?
a) The Cavern Club
b) The Marquee Club
c) Ronnie Scott's Jazz Club
d) The Roundhouse

The Escorts (Answers)

254. b) Terry Sylvester
255. c) "All Over Now"
256. b) Graham Nash
257. d) Merseybeat
258. d) "The Escorts"

The Eyes (Answers)

259. a) The Spectacles
260. c) The Marquee Club
261. d) Chris Lovegrove
262. b) "I'm Rowed Out"
263. c) Wally Waller
264. a) "The Eyes"
265. d) Personal commitments

Fairport Convention (Answers)

266. c) Simon Nicol
267. c) Folk Rock
268. b) "Tam Lin"
269. c) Sandy Denny
270. c) Cropredy Festival
271. a) Plane crash (drummer Martin Lamble and Richard Thompson's then-girlfriend Jeannie Franklyn lost their lives)

Georgie Fame (& The Blue Flames) (Answers)

272. c) Georgie Fame
273. c) Organ
274. c) Van Morrison
275. d) "Two Faces of Fame"
276. d) Rhythm and Blues
277. c) Ronnie Scott's Jazz Club

Finders Keepers (Answers Page 73)

278. In what year was the British rock band Finders Keepers
formed?
a) 1963
b) 1965
c) 1967
d) 1969

279. Which member of Finders Keepers later gained fame as a
keyboardist and songwriter for the progressive rock band
Yes?
a) Tony Kaye
b) Rick Wakeman
c) Geoff Downes
d) Patrick Moraz

280. Finders Keepers contributed music to which British film
directed by Michael Reeves?
a) "Alfie"
b) "The Wicker Man"
c) "Witchfinder General"
d) "If...."

281. What was the title of Finders Keepers' debut album, released
in 1966?
a) "Lost and Found"
b) "Finders Keepers"
c) "Now and Then"
d) "Time Capsule"

282. Finders Keepers was known for their lively stage
performances and often appeared on which popular British
music television show?
a) Ready Steady Go!
b) Top of the Pops
c) The Ed Sullivan Show
d) Shindig!

Fleetwood Mac (Answers Page 73)

283. Who is the co-founder and drummer of Fleetwood Mac?
    a) Lindsey Buckingham
    b) Mick Fleetwood
    c) Stevie Nicks
    d) Christine McVie

284. Fleetwood Mac's debut album, released in 1968, is titled:
    a) "Fleetwood Mac"
    b) "Then Play On"
    c) "Rumours"
    d) "Tusk"

285. Who joined Fleetwood Mac as a guitarist and vocalist in
    1975, contributing to the band's commercial success?
    a) Peter Green
    b) Lindsey Buckingham
    c) Danny Kirwan
    d) Bob Welch

286. Which Fleetwood Mac song, released in 1968, became a hit
    in the UK and is known for its distinctive guitar riff?
    a) "Rhiannon"
    b) "Oh Well"
    c) "Go Your Own Way"
    d) "The Chain"

287. Fleetwood Mac's album "Rumours," released in 1977,
    includes the hit singles "Go Your Own Way" and:
    a) "Landslide"
    b) "Rhiannon"
    c) "Dreams"
    d) "Don't Stop"

288. Who is the lead vocalist and one of the primary songwriters
    for Fleetwood Mac?
    a) Mick Fleetwood
    b) Christine McVie
    c) Stevie Nicks
    d) John McVie

Fleetwood Mac (Answers Page 73)

289. In 1969, Fleetwood Mac released an instrumental track that became one of their signature songs. What is the title?
a) "Albatross"
b) "Black Magic Woman"
c) "The Chain"
d) "Sara"

290. Fleetwood Mac's album "Tusk," released in 1979, is notable for experimenting with which unconventional musical elements?
a) Symphonic arrangements
b) Electronic dance music
c) Reggae influences
d) Punk rock

The Fortunes (Answers Page 73)

291. The Fortunes, a 1960s British rock band, had a hit single with the song "You've Got Your Troubles." In what year was this song released?
a) 1962
b) 1964
c) 1966
d) 1968

292. What city served as the hometown for The Fortunes during their early years in the music industry?
a) Liverpool
b) Manchester
c) Birmingham
d) London

293. The Fortunes gained international success with their hit "Here It Comes Again." What was the peak position of this single on the UK Singles Chart?
a) #1
b) #5
c) #10
d) #15

The Fortunes (Answers Page 73)

294. Which member of The Fortunes co-wrote the song "Storm in a Teacup," which became one of their notable hits in the 1970s?
a) Barry Pritchard
b) Glen Dale
c) Rod Allen
d) Shel MacRae

295. The Fortunes achieved success in the United States with the single "You've Got Your Troubles." What position did it reach on the Billboard Hot 100 chart?
a) #7
b) #15
c) #20
d) #30

296. The Fortunes released a cover of a classic song that became one of their hits in the 1960s. What is the title of this song?
a) "Unchained Melody"
b) "A Groovy Kind of Love"
c) "You Don't Know Like I Know"
d) "I'm Gonna Make You Love Me"

297. The Fortunes' original lineup included three vocalists. Which member became the lead vocalist after the departure of Shel MacRae?
a) Barry Pritchard
b) Glen Dale
c) Rod Allen
d) Mike Smith

Wayne Fontana & The Mindbenders
(Answers Page 73)

298. What was the name of Wayne Fontana and the Mindbenders' first hit single?
a) "Um, Um, Um, Um, Um, Um"
b) "The Game of Love"
c) "A Groovy Kind of Love"

d) "It's Just a Little Bit Too Late"
Wayne Fontana & The Mindbenders
(Answers Page 73)

299. Who was the lead singer of Wayne Fontana and the
Mindbenders?
a) Wayne Fontana
b) Bob Lang
c) Ric Rothwell
d) Eric Stewart

300. Which Wayne Fontana and the Mindbenders song topped
the UK charts in 1965?
a) "Um, Um, Um, Um, Um, Um"
b) "The Game of Love"
c) "A Groovy Kind of Love"
d) "It's Just a Little Bit Too Late"

301. Who played drums on Wayne Fontana and the
Mindbenders' 1965 hit "The Game of Love"?
a) Bob Lang
b) Ric Rothwell
c) Eric Stewart
d) Kevin Godley

302. Which Wayne Fontana and the Mindbenders song was
covered by Phil Collins in 1982?
a) "Um, Um, Um, Um, Um, Um"
b) "The Game of Love"
c) "A Groovy Kind of Love"
d) "It's Just a Little Bit Too Late"

303. Who played bass guitar on Wayne Fontana and the
Mindbenders' 1965 hit "The Game of Love"?
a) Bob Lang
b) Ric Rothwell
c) Eric Stewart
d) Graham Gouldman

Finders Keepers (Answers)

278. b) 1965
279. b) Rick Wakeman
280. c) "Witchfinder General"
281. a) "Lost and Found"
282. b) Top of the Pops

Fleetwood Mac (Answers)

283. b) Mick Fleetwood
284. a) "Fleetwood Mac"
285. b) Lindsey Buckingham
286. b) "Oh Well"
287. c) "Dreams"
288. c) Stevie Nicks
289. a) "Albatross"
290. a) Symphonic arrangements

The Fortunes (Answers)

291. c) 1966
292. b) Manchester
293. b) #5
294. a) Barry Pritchard
295. a) #7
296. b) "A Groovy Kind of Love"
297. c) Rod Allen

Wayne Fontana & The Mindbenders (Answers)

298. a) "Um, Um, Um, Um, Um, Um"
299. a) Wayne Fontana
300. b) "The Game of Love"
301. b) Ric Rothwell
302. c) "A Groovy Kind of Love"
303. d) Graham Gouldman

The Fourmost (Answers Page 80)

304. What was the original name of the 1960s British rock band "The Fourmost" before they changed it to The Fourmost?
a) The Merseybeats
b) The Mavericks
c) The Escorts
d) The Beatles

305. The Fourmost gained popularity as part of the Merseybeat sound in Liverpool. Which legendary British rock band played a significant role in their early success?
a) The Rolling Stones
b) The Who
c) The Kinks
d) The Beatles

306. What was the title of The Fourmost's debut single, released in 1963, which became a hit in the UK?
a) "A Little Loving"
b) "Hello Little Girl"
c) "I'm in Love"
d) "How Can I Tell Her"

307. The Fourmost had another hit single in 1964 that reached the UK Top 10. What is the title of this song?
a) "A Little Loving"
b) "Baby I Need Your Lovin'"
c) "I'm in Love"
d) "Here, There and Everywhere"

308. Who was the lead singer and rhythm guitarist of The Fourmost?
a) Billy Hatton
b) Mike Millward
c) Dave Lovelady
d) Brian O'Hara

The Fourmost (Answers Page 80)

309. The Fourmost toured with The Beatles during the early
1960s. What was the name of The Fourmost's manager, who
also managed The Beatles?
a) Brian Epstein
b) Andrew Loog Oldham
c) Kit Lambert
d) Peter Grant

Peter Frampton (Answers Page 80)

310. What was the name of Peter Frampton's band before he
embarked on his solo career in the 1970s?
a) The Herd
b) The Zombies
c) The Yardbirds
d) The Troggs

311. Which instrumental track from Peter Frampton's album
"Frampton Comes Alive!" became a massive hit in 1976?
a) "Show Me the Way"
b) "Baby, I Love Your Way"
c) "Do You Feel Like We Do"
d) "Lines on My Face"

312. Peter Frampton played the lead guitar on which classic rock
album by another famous artist in the 1970s?
a) "The Dark Side of the Moon" by Pink Floyd
b) "A Night at the Opera" by Queen
c) "Hotel California" by Eagles
d) "Sticky Fingers" by The Rolling Stones

313. Which Peter Frampton album, released in 1973, featured the
hit single "Show Me the Way"?
a) "Frampton Comes Alive!"
b) "I'm in You"
c) "Wind of Change"
d) "Frampton's Camel"

Peter Frampton (Answers Page 80)

314. In 1968, Peter Frampton briefly joined a supergroup that
included Steve Marriott. What was the name of this band?
a) Blind Faith
b) Humble Pie
c) The Jeff Beck Group
d) Cream

315. What was the title of Peter Frampton's debut solo album,
released in 1972?
a) "Frampton's Camel"
b) "Somethin's Happening"
c) "Wind of Change"
d) "Peter Frampton"

316. Peter Frampton gained international fame with his live
album "Frampton Comes Alive!" Which city was the primary
location for the recording of this album?
a) New York City
b) Los Angeles
c) Chicago
d) San Francisco

317. What is the name of the talk box, an effects device
frequently used by Peter Frampton to create his distinctive
sound?
a) Wah-wah pedal
b) Leslie speaker
c) Echoplex
d) Vocoder

318. In 1978, Peter Frampton starred in a musical comedy film
alongside The Bee Gees. What is the title of this film?
a) "Grease"
b) "Saturday Night Fever"
c) "Sgt. Pepper's Lonely Hearts Club Band"
d) "The Rocky Horror Picture Show"

Freddie & The Dreamers (Answers Page 80)

319. Which hit song by Freddie and the Dreamers topped the
UK Singles Chart in 1963 and also achieved success in the
United States?
a) "Do Wah Diddy Diddy"
b) "I'm Telling You Now"
c) "Glad All Over"
d) "A World Without Love"

320. Freddie and the Dreamers gained popularity for a distinctive
dance associated with their performances. What was the
name of this dance?
a) The Twist
b) The Mashed Potato
c) The Freddie
d) The Locomotion

321. Which city in England was Freddie and the Dreamers
originally formed in?
a) Liverpool
b) Manchester
c) London
d) Birmingham

322. In 1965, Freddie and the Dreamers appeared in a musical
comedy film. What is the title of this film?
a) A Hard Day's Night
b) Help!
c) Ferry Cross the Mersey
d) Every Day's a Holiday

323. Who was the lead singer and frontman of Freddie and the
Dreamers?
a) Freddie Marsden
b) Freddie Garrity
c) Freddie Mercury
d) Freddie and the Dreamers had multiple lead singers

Freddie & The Dreamers (Answers Page 80)

324. Which American TV show did Freddie and the Dreamers make several appearances on during the mid-1960s, contributing to their international fame?
a) The Ed Sullivan Show
b) The Tonight Show Starring Johnny Carson
c) American Bandstand
d) The Dick Van Dyke Show

Free (Answers Page 80)

325. Which of the following is NOT a member of Free?
a) Paul Rodgers
b) Andy Fraser
c) Mick Jagger
d) Paul Kossoff

326. What was Free's breakthrough hit single, released in 1968, that became an anthem for the counterculture movement?
a) "All Right Now"
b) "Wishing Well"
c) "Fire and Water"
d) "My Brother Jake"

327. Free's fourth studio album, released in 1970, is titled:
a) "Free at Last"
b) "Fire and Water"
c) "Highway"
d) "Heartbreaker"

328. Which member of Free later joined Bad Company with Paul Rodgers?
a) Andy Fraser
b) Paul Kossoff
c) Simon Kirke
d) Paul Rodgers

Free (Answers Page 80)

329. What was the last studio album released by Free before they disbanded in 1973?
a) "Free"
b) "Heartbreaker"
c) "Highway"
d) "Fire and Water"

330. Free's guitarist Paul Kossoff played a famous 1959 Gibson Les Paul. What nickname did he give to his guitar?
a) Black Beauty
b) Old Yeller
c) Green Meanie
d) Brownie

331. Which Free album features the hit song "All Right Now"?
a) "Tons of Sobs"
b) "Fire and Water"
c) "Highway"
d) "Free"

The Fourmost (Answers)

304. c) The Escorts
305. d) The Beatles
306. b) "Hello Little Girl"
307. a) "A Little Loving"
308. a) Billy Hatton
309. a) Brian Epstein

Peter Frampton (Answers)

310. a) The Herd
311. c) "Do You Feel Like We Do"
312. a) "The Dark Side of the Moon" by Pink Floyd
313. c) "Wind of Change"
314. b) Humble Pie
315. b) "Somethin's Happening"
316. d) San Francisco
317. d) Vocoder
318. c) "Sgt. Pepper's Lonely Hearts Club Band

Freddie & The Dreamers (Answers)

319. b) "I'm Telling You Now"
320. c) The Freddie
321. b) Manchester
322. d) Every Day's a Holiday
323. b) Freddie Garrity
324. a) The Ed Sullivan Show

Free (Answers)

325. c) Mick Jagger
326. d) "My Brother Jake"
327. a) "Free at Last"
328. c) Simon Kirke
329. b) "Heartbreaker"
330. c) Green Meanie
331. b) "Fire and Water"

Billy Fury (Answers Page 87)

332. What was Billy Fury's real name?
    a) Ronald Wycherley
    b) John Lennon
    c) Tommy Steele
    d) Cliff Richard

333. Which of the following was one of Billy Fury's hit singles in the 1960s?
    a) "Lucille"
    b) "Peggy Sue"
    c) "C'mon Everybody"
    d) "Halfway to Paradise"

334. In which year did Billy Fury release his debut album, "The Sound of Fury"?
    a) 1958
    b) 1961
    c) 1963
    d) 1965

335. Which instrument did Billy Fury primarily play?
    a) Guitar
    b) Piano
    c) Drums
    d) Saxophone

336. What was the title of Billy Fury's first UK number-one hit single?
    a) "Jealousy"
    b) "Wondrous Place"
    c) "Halfway to Paradise"
    d) "Last Night Was Made for Love"

337. Which famous rock and roll impresario and manager discovered Billy Fury?
    a) Brian Epstein
    b) Larry Parnes
    c) Phil Spector

d) Andrew Loog Oldham

Billy Fury (Answers Page 87)

338. What was the title of Billy Fury's first studio album, released in 1960?
a) "The Sound of Fury"
b) "Billy Fury"
c) "Halfway to Paradise"
d) "Wondrous Place"

339. Which film starred Billy Fury in the lead role and was released in 1962?
a) "That'll Be the Day"
b) "The Young Ones"
c) "Play It Cool"
d) "Summer Holiday"

340. Who was Billy Fury's longtime backing band in the 1960s?
a) The Shadows
b) The Crickets
c) The Tornados
d) The Blue Flames

341. Which American rock and roll legend influenced Billy Fury's musical style?
a) Elvis Presley
b) Buddy Holly
c) Chuck Berry
d) Little Richard

342. What was Billy Fury's highest-charting single in the UK, reaching number three in 1961?
a) "Last Night Was Made for Love"
b) "A Thousand Stars"
c) "I'd Never Find Another You"
d) "Jealousy"

343. In which year did Billy Fury receive an Ivor Novello Award for "Halfway to Paradise"?
a) 1958
b) 1961

c) 1963
d) 1965

Billy Fury (Answers Page 87)

344. What medical condition did Billy Fury struggle with
throughout his life?
a) Diabetes
b) Asthma
c) Heart disease
d) Epilepsy

345. Which of the following artists covered Billy Fury's song
"Halfway to Paradise" in 1961?
a) Cliff Richard
b) Bobby Vee
c) Neil Sedaka
d) Tony Orlando

346. What was the title of Billy Fury's final studio album, released
in 1982 shortly before his death?
a) "The Sound of Fury"
b) "Billy Fury"
c) "The Final Recordings"
d) "One Kiss"

Genesis (Answers Page 87)

347. Who was the original lead singer of the 1960s British rock
band Genesis?
a) Peter Gabriel
b) Phil Collins
c) Tony Banks
d) Mike Rutherford

348. In 1967, Genesis released their debut album. What is the
title of this album?
a) "Nursery Cryme"
b) "From Genesis to Revelation"
c) "Trespass"
d) "Foxtrot"

Genesis (Answers Page 87)

349. Which member of Genesis became the lead vocalist after Peter Gabriel's departure in 1975?
a) Mike Rutherford
b) Steve Hackett
c) Tony Banks
d) Phil Collins

350. What was the name of the concept album released by Genesis in 1974, featuring the epic song "Supper's Ready"?
a) "The Lamb Lies Down on Broadway"
b) "Selling England by the Pound"
c) "Nursery Cryme"
d) "A Trick of the Tail"

351. Which progressive rock era album by Genesis includes the track "Watcher of the Skies"?
a) "Wind & Wuthering"
b) "Foxtrot"
c) "Genesis Live"
d) "Duke"

352. In 1969, who replaced John Silver as the drummer for Genesis, marking the beginning of the classic lineup?
a) Phil Collins
b) Chester Thompson
c) Bill Bruford
d) Steve Hackett

353. What was the title of Genesis's breakthrough album, released in 1973, which included the hit single "I Know What I Like (In Your Wardrobe)"?
a) "Nursery Cryme"
b) "A Trick of the Tail"
c) "Selling England by the Pound"
d) "Duke"

Gerry And The Pacemakers (Answers Page 87)

354. Who was the lead singer and founder of the 1960s British rock band Gerry and the Pacemakers?
a) Gerry Anderson
b) Gerry Marsden
c) Gerry Harrison
d) Gerry Smith

355. Which Gerry and the Pacemakers hit single became an anthem for the city of Liverpool and is often sung by football fans at Anfield, the home of Liverpool FC?
a) "Ferry Cross the Mersey"
b) "How Do You Do It?"
c) "You'll Never Walk Alone"
d) "Don't Let the Sun Catch You Crying"

356. In 1963, Gerry and the Pacemakers achieved their first number-one single in the UK charts. What was the title of this song?
a) "I Like It"
b) "It's All Right"
c) "I'm the One"
d) "Don't Let the Sun Catch You Crying"

357. Gerry and the Pacemakers' second single, released in 1963, also reached number one in the UK. What was the title of this hit song?
a) "How Do You Do It?"
b) "You'll Never Walk Alone"
c) "I'm the One"
d) "Ferry Cross the Mersey"

358. What was the name of Gerry and the Pacemakers' debut album, released in 1964?
a) "Gerry's Hits"
b) "How Do You Do It?"
c) "Ferry Cross the Mersey"
d) "Don't Let the Sun Catch You Crying"

Gerry And The Pacemakers (Answers Page 87)

359. Which famous American television variety show did Gerry
and the Pacemakers appear on during the 1960s, contributing
to their international fame?
a) The Ed Sullivan Show
b) The Tonight Show Starring Johnny Carson
c) American Bandstand
d) The Dick Van Dyke Show

360. Gerry and the Pacemakers were part of the Merseybeat
movement. Which city is often associated with this musical
scene?
a) Manchester
b) Birmingham
c) Liverpool
d) London

361. What was the final Gerry and the Pacemakers single released
before they disbanded in 1966?
a) "Girl on a Swing"
b) "Give All Your Love to Me"
c) "I'll Wait for You"
d) "Without You"

Billy Fury (Answers)

332. a) Ronald Wycherley
333. d) "Halfway to Paradise"
334. b) 1961
335. a) Guitar
336. a) "Jealousy"
337. b) Larry Parnes
338. b) "Billy Fury"
339. c) "Play It Cool"
340. d) The Blue Flames
341. b) Buddy Holly
342. a) "Last Night Was Made for Love"
343. b) 1961
344. d) Epilepsy
345. c) Neil Sedaka
346. c) "The Final Recordings"

Genesis (Answers)

347. a) Peter Gabriel
348. b) "From Genesis to Revelation"
349. d) Phil Collins
350. a) "The Lamb Lies Down on Broadway"
351. b) "Foxtrot"
352. a) Phil Collins
353. c) "Selling England by the Pound"

Gerry And The Pacemakers (Answers)

354. b) Gerry Marsden
355. c) "You'll Never Walk Alone"
356. a) "I Like It"
357. d) "Ferry Cross the Mersey
358. d) "Don't Let the Sun Catch You Crying"
359. a) The Ed Sullivan Show
360. c) Liverpool
361. a) "Girl on a Swing"

The Gods (Answers Page 93)

362. The Gods were a British rock band that emerged in the 1960s. Which member of the band later gained fame as the guitarist for Deep Purple?
a) Mick Taylor
b) Ritchie Blackmore
c) Eric Clapton
d) Jimmy Page

363. Before adopting the name "The Gods," the band was initially known by another name. What was their original moniker?
a) The Rolling Stones
b) The Yardbirds
c) The Human Instinct
d) The Crawdaddies

364. The Gods' music style evolved over time. What genre was the band primarily associated with during its early years?
a) Psychedelic rock
b) Blues rock
c) Progressive rock
d) Folk rock

365. In 1968, The Gods released an album that is considered a milestone in the progressive rock genre. What is the title of this influential album?
a) "Genesis"
b) "To Samuel a Son"
c) "Electricity"
d) "Contact High with the Gods"

366. Which member of The Gods went on to have a successful solo career and became known for his work as a session guitarist with artists like Elton John and George Harrison?
a) Ken Hensley
b) Mick Taylor
c) Greg Lake
d) Peter Frampton

The Gods (Answers Page 93)

367. The Gods were part of the British blues scene in the 1960s.
Which blues legend did they support on tour during their
early years?
a) B.B. King
b) Muddy Waters
c) John Lee Hooker
d) Howlin' Wolf

368. The Gods experienced several lineup changes during their
existence. Which musician served as the lead vocalist for the
band in its later years?
a) Mick Taylor
b) John Glascock
c) Keith Relf
d) Cliff Bennett

Gong (Answers Page 93)

369. Who is the founding member and lead vocalist of Gong?
a) Daevid Allen
b) Steve Hillage
c) Pierre Moerlen
d) Gilli Smyth

370. Gong's debut album, released in 1971, is titled:
a) "Flying Teapot"
b) "Angel's Egg"
c) "You"
d) "Camembert Electrique"

371. What unique style of music is often associated with Gong?
a) Space rock
b) Reggae
c) Glam rock
d) Punk rock

Gong (Answers Page 93)

372. Daevid Allen was previously a member of another influential psychedelic rock band before founding Gong. What was the name of that band?
a) Soft Machine
b) Pink Floyd
c) The Incredible String Band
d) The Nice

373. Gong's mythology features a character known as the "Pot Head Pixies." What album prominently features this concept?
a) "You"
b) "Angels Egg"
c) "Shamal"
d) "Flying Teapot"

Gun (Answers Page 93)

374. Who was the lead vocalist and founding member of the band Gun?
a) Adrian Gurvitz
b) Paul Gurvitz
c) Mick Moody
d) Louie Farrell

375. Gun is best known for their 1968 hit single:
a) "Sunshine of Your Love"
b) "Race with the Devil"
c) "White Room"
d) "Purple Haze"

376. Which genre is often associated with Gun's music?
a) Psychedelic rock
b) Blues rock
c) Progressive rock
d) Folk rock

Gun (Answers Page 93)

377. In 1968, Gun released their debut album. What was the title
of this album?
a) "Gun"
b) "Race with the Devil"
c) "Taking on the World"
d) "Gallagher and Lyle"

378. Gun underwent a lineup change in the early 1970s. Which
member of the band later joined the Moody Blues?
a) Adrian Gurvitz
b) Paul Gurvitz
c) Louie Farrell
d) Steve Winwood

Hawkwind (Answers Page 93)

379. Who is the founding member and lead vocalist of
Hawkwind?
a) Dave Brock
b) Lemmy Kilmister
c) Nik Turner
d) Robert Calvert

380. Hawkwind's classic 1972 album, often considered a
landmark in space rock, is titled:
a) "Hall of the Mountain Grill"
b) "Warrior on the Edge of Time"
c) "In Search of Space"
d) "Doremi Fasol Latido"

381. Prior to forming Hawkwind, Dave Brock and other
members were part of a London-based band known as:
a) Pink Fairies
b) Gong
c) The Deviants
d) Man

Hawkwind (Answers Page 93)

382. Which famous Motörhead member played bass for
Hawkwind before forming his own band?
a) Phil Taylor
b) Lemmy Kilmister
c) Eddie Clarke
d) Philthy Animal Taylor

383. Hawkwind's single "Silver Machine," featuring Lemmy on
vocals, became a hit in 1972. Who wrote this song?
a) Dave Brock
b) Nik Turner
c) Robert Calvert
d) Lemmy Kilmister

The Gods (Answers)

362. b) Ritchie Blackmore
363. d) The Crawdaddies
364. b) Blues rock
365. c) "Electricity"
366. a) Ken Hensley
367. c) John Lee Hooker
368. b) John Glascock

Gong (Answers)

369. a) Daevid Allen
370. d) "Camembert Electrique"
371. a) Space rock
372. a) Soft Machine
373. b) "Angels Egg"

Gun (Answers)

374. a) Adrian Gurvitz
375. b) "Race with the Devil"
376. a) Psychedelic rock
377. a) "Gun"
378. b) Paul Gurvitz

Hawkwind (Answers)

379. a) Dave Brock
380. b) "Warrior on the Edge of Time"
381. c) The Deviants
382. b) Lemmy Kilmister
383. a) Dave Brock

Hedgehoppers Anonymous (Answers Page 99)

384. What was the debut single that brought the 1960s British
rock band Hedgehoppers Anonymous to fame in 1965?
a) "Sunny Afternoon"
b) "Time of the Season"
c) "It's Good News Week"
d) "Friday on My Mind"

385. Which city in England was Hedgehoppers Anonymous
originally formed in?
a) Manchester
b) Liverpool
c) Birmingham
d) Cambridge

386. In 1965, Hedgehoppers Anonymous released their first and
only studio album. What is the title of this album?
a) "Hoppin' Around"
b) "The Sound of Music"
c) "Hedgehopping"
d) "It's Good News Week"

387. What was the inspiration for the name "Hedgehoppers
Anonymous"?
a) A popular comic strip
b) A local wildlife club
c) A TV sitcom
d) A children's book

388. Which music genre is most closely associated with
Hedgehoppers Anonymous?
a) Psychedelic Rock
b) Folk Rock
c) Merseybeat
d) Beat music

The Herd (Answers Page 99)

389. The Herd, a British rock band of the 1960s, featured a lead singer who later became a prominent solo artist. What is the name of this singer?
a) Peter Frampton
b) Gary Glitter
c) Steve Marriott
d) Peter Noone

390. Before Peter Frampton joined The Herd, who was the band's original lead vocalist?
a) Andy Bown
b) Gary Taylor
c) Terry Clark
d) Andy Steele

391. The Herd had a hit single in 1967 with a cover of a song originally by Bob Dylan. What is the title of this song?
a) "I Don't Want Our Loving to Die"
b) "From the Underworld"
c) "Sunshine Cottage"
d) "Paradise Lost"

392. What was the name of The Herd's debut album, released in 1967?
a) "Paradise Lost"
b) "From the Underworld"
c) "The Herd Strikes Again"
d) "Goodbye Baby, Hello Friend"

393. The Herd's hit single "From the Underworld" reached the Top 10 in the UK charts. What was its highest chart position?
a) #4
b) #6
c) #8
d) #10

The Herd (Answers Page 99)

394. Which member of The Herd later joined the rock band
Uriah Heep and became known for his keyboard skills?
a) Andy Bown
b) Gary Taylor
c) Peter Frampton
d) Andy Steele

395. The Herd disbanded in 1968, and Peter Frampton pursued a
successful solo career. What was the title of Peter Frampton's
breakthrough solo album released in 1976?
a) "Frampton's Camel"
b) "I'm in You"
c) "Frampton Comes Alive!"
d) "Wind of Change"

Hermans Hermits (Answers Page 99)

396. Who was the lead singer and frontman of the 1960s British
rock band Herman's Hermits?
a) Herman Munster
b) Herman Smith
c) Herman Goering
d) Peter Noone

397. Herman's Hermits achieved international success with their
debut single. What is the title of this hit song released in
1964?
a) "Mrs. Brown, You've Got a Lovely Daughter"
b) "There's a Kind of Hush"
c) "I'm Into Something Good"
d) "No Milk Today"

398. In 1965, Herman's Hermits starred in a musical comedy film
that shares its title with one of their popular songs. What is
the title of the film?
a) "Hold On!"
b) "A Hard Day's Night"

c) "Help!"
d) "Mrs. Brown, You've Got a Lovely Daughter"

Hermans Hermits (Answers Page 99)

399. Which member of Herman's Hermits played the role of
Herman in the band's name but was not the lead singer?
a) Derek Leckenby
b) Barry Whitwam
c) Karl Green
d) Keith Hopwood

400. What was the title of Herman's Hermits' second studio
album, released in 1965, featuring hits like "Can't You Hear
My Heartbeat" and "Silhouettes"?
a) "Blaze"
b) "Both Sides of Herman's Hermits"
c) "Mrs. Brown, You've Got a Lovely Daughter"
d) "The Best of Herman's Hermits"

401. Which Herman's Hermits hit single released in 1966 reached
number two on the US Billboard Hot 100?
a) "I'm Henry VIII, I Am"
b) "There's a Kind of Hush"
c) "Dandy"
d) "I'm Into Something Good"

402. What was the name of Herman's Hermits' manager who
played a crucial role in the band's success during the 1960s?
a) Brian Epstein
b) Andrew Loog Oldham
c) Mickey Most
d) Larry Parnes

403. Herman's Hermits had a hit with a cover of a song originally
recorded by The Kinks. What is the title of this song?
a) "My Generation"
b) "Dandy"
c) "Bus Stop"
d) "No Milk Today"

Hermans Hermits (Answers Page 99)

404. In 1967, Herman's Hermits released an album with a title referencing a famous British television series. What is the title of this album?
a) "The Avengers"
b) "Doctor Who"
c) "The Prisoner"
d) "Both Sides of Herman's Hermits"

405. What was the last top 10 hit for Herman's Hermits in the US, released in 1967?
a) "There's a Kind of Hush"
b) "No Milk Today"
c) "I Can Take or Leave Your Loving"
d) "Something's Happening"

Hedgehoppers Anonymous (Answers)

384. c) "It's Good News Week"
385. d) Cambridge
386. c) "Hedgehopping"
387. b) A local wildlife club
388. d) Beat music

The Herd (Answers)

389. a) Peter Frampton
390. d) Andy Steele
391. a) "I Don't Want Our Loving to Die"
392. c) "The Herd Strikes Again"
393. c) #8
394. a) Andy Bown
395. c) "Frampton Comes Alive!"

Hermans Hermits (Answers)

396. d) Peter Noone
397. c) "I'm Into Something Good
398. a) "Hold On!"
399. b) Barry Whitwam
400. a) "Blaze"
401. a) "I'm Henry VIII, I Am"
402. c) Mickey Most
403. b) "Dandy"
404. a) "The Avengers"
405. a) "There's a Kind of Hush"

The Hollies (Answers Page 105)

406. Who were the founding members of The Hollies?
    a) Graham Nash, Allan Clarke, and Tony Hicks
    b) Eric Clapton, Mick Jagger, and Keith Richards
    c) John Lennon, Paul McCartney, and George Harrison
    d) Roger Daltrey, Pete Townshend, and John Entwistle

407. The Hollies released their debut single in 1963, which was a cover of a classic song. What was the title of this single?
    a) "Bus Stop"
    b) "Carrie-Anne"
    c) "Just One Look"
    d) "Searchin'"

408. In 1966, The Hollies had a major international hit with the song "Bus Stop." Who wrote this iconic track?
    a) Ray Davies
    b) Gerry Goffin and Carole King
    c) Lennon-McCartney
    d) Graham Gouldman

409. What was the title of The Hollies' 1969 album that featured the hit song "He Ain't Heavy, He's My Brother"?
    a) "Evolution"
    b) "Butterfly"
    c) "Distant Light"
    d) "Hollies Sing Hollies"

410. Which member of The Hollies had a successful solo career after leaving the band, with hits like "On a Carousel"?
    a) Graham Nash
    b) Allan Clarke
    c) Tony Hicks
    d) Bobby Elliott

411. The Hollies had a significant influence on the British Invasion. What city did the band originate from?
    a) Manchester

b) Liverpool
c) London
d) Birmingham

The Hollies (Answers Page 105)

412. In 1967, The Hollies released an album featuring the hit
single "Carrie-Anne." What is the title of this album?
a) "For Certain Because..."
b) "Stay with The Hollies"
c) "Butterfly"
d) "Dear Eloise/King Midas in Reverse"

413. Which Hollies song, released in 1974, became a chart-
topping hit in the United States?
a) "Long Cool Woman (in a Black Dress)"
b) "The Air That I Breathe"
c) "Stop! Stop! Stop!"
d) "He Ain't Heavy, He's My Brother"

414. The Hollies were known for their covers of American rock
and roll songs. Which Buddy Holly song did they cover and
release as a single in 1963?
a) "That'll Be the Day"
b) "Peggy Sue"
c) "Not Fade Away"
d) "Maybe Baby"

The Honeycombs (Answers Page 105)

415. Who was the lead vocalist of the 1960s British rock band
The Honeycombs?
a) Dennis D'Ell
b) Marianne Faithfull
c) Honey Lantree
d) Joe Meek

416. The Honeycombs had a breakthrough hit in 1964 with a
song that reached the top 10 in both the UK and the US.
What is the title of this hit single?
a) "Have I the Right?"
b) "Da Doo Ron Ron"
c) "He's a Rebel"

d) "Twist and Shout"

The Honeycombs (Answers Page 105)

417. What was distinctive about The Honeycombs' lineup in terms of gender roles, setting them apart from other bands of the era?
a) All-female members
b) All-male members
c) Equal gender representation
d) Only instrumentalists, no vocalists

418. Which member of The Honeycombs played the unusual instrument called the "honey-tone" or "marxophone" in their performances and recordings?
a) Martin Murray
b) Alan Ward
c) Honey Lantree
d) John Lantree

419. The Honeycombs were associated with a notable record producer who played a significant role in shaping their sound. What is the name of this producer?
a) George Martin
b) Phil Spector
c) Joe Meek
d) Brian Epstein

420. The Honeycombs' second single, released in 1965, failed to replicate the success of their debut. What is the title of this less successful single?
a) "That's the Way"
b) "Something Better Beginning"
c) "I Can't Stop"
d) "Colour Slide"

421. What was the final single released by The Honeycombs before they disbanded in 1966?
a) "This Year, Next Year"
b) "Eyes"
c) "Love in Tokyo"

d) "I Can't Stop"

Jethro Tull (Answers Page 105)

422. Who is the founder and frontman of the 1960s British rock
band Jethro Tull?
a) Ian Anderson
b) Robert Plant
c) Roger Waters
d) Ian Gillan

423. Jethro Tull is often associated with the distinctive use of
which instrument, played by Ian Anderson, that is not
typically featured in rock music?
a) Saxophone
b) Flute
c) Violin
d) Banjo

424. Which Jethro Tull album, released in 1969, is considered a
seminal work in the progressive rock genre and features the
iconic track "Aqualung"?
a) "Stand Up"
b) "Thick as a Brick"
c) "Aqualung"
d) "Benefit"

425. What was the original name of Jethro Tull's debut album,
released in 1968, before being changed to "This Was"?
a) "Songs from the Wood"
b) "Tull Tales"
c) "The Jethro Tull Experience"
d) "Blues in G"

426. Which Jethro Tull album, released in 1972, is a concept
album with a continuous piece of music on both sides and is
known for its intricate cover design?
a) "Thick as a Brick"
b) "A Passion Play"
c) "War Child"
d) "Minstrel in the Gallery"

Jethro Tull (Answers Page 105)

427. Jethro Tull won the inaugural Grammy Award for Best Hard Rock/Metal Performance in 1989. Which album earned them this recognition?
a) "Aqualung"
b) "Heavy Horses"
c) "Crest of a Knave"
d) "Songs from the Wood"

428. Which member of Jethro Tull is known for his distinctive stage presence, often standing on one leg while playing the flute?
a) Martin Barre
b) John Evan
c) Jeffrey Hammond
d) Ian Anderson

429. Jethro Tull's album "War Child" was released in 1974 and was accompanied by a short film. Who directed this film?
a) Stanley Kubrick
b) Martin Scorsese
c) David Lynch
d) Sam Peckinpah

430. Which Jethro Tull album, released in 1977, is a concept album exploring the themes of the changing seasons?
a) "Heavy Horses"
b) "Songs from the Wood"
c) "Minstrel in the Gallery"
d) "Stormwatch"

431. Jethro Tull's name is derived from an 18th-century agriculturalist. What did this historical figure invent?
a) Seed drill
b) Plow
c) Crop rotation
d) Threshing machine

The Hollies (Answers)

406. a) Graham Nash, Allan Clarke, and Tony Hicks
407. c) "Just One Look"
408. d) Graham Gouldman
409. c) "Distant Light"
410. b) Allan Clarke
411. a) Manchester
412. c) "Butterfly"
413. b) "The Air That I Breathe
414. c) "Not Fade Away"

The Honeycombs (Answers)

415. c) Honey Lantree
416. a) "Have I the Right?"
417. a) All-female members
418. d) John Lantree
419. c) Joe Meek
420. b) "Something Better Beginning"
421. c) "Love in Tokyo"

Jethro Tull (Answers)

422. a) Ian Anderson
423. b) Flute
424. c) "Aqualung"
425. b) "Tull Tales"
426. b) "A Passion Play"
427. c) "Crest of a Knave"
428. d) Ian Anderson
429. a) Stanley Kubrick
430. b) "Songs from the Wood"
431. a) Seed drill

Johnny Kidd & The Pirates (Answers Page 111)

432. Who was the lead singer and frontman of the 1960s British rock band Johnny Kidd and the Pirates?
a) Johnny Depp
b) Johnny Kidd
c) Johnny Rotten
d) Johnny Cash

433. Johnny Kidd and the Pirates had a major hit in 1960 with a song that features a distinctive stomping beat. What is the title of this hit single?
a) "Shakin' All Over"
b) "Summertime Blues"
c) "Twist and Shout"
d) "Great Balls of Fire"

434. Which British music variety show provided Johnny Kidd and the Pirates with a platform to perform their hit "Shakin' All Over" in 1960, propelling them to fame?
a) Ready Steady Go!
b) Top of the Pops
c) The Ed Sullivan Show
d) Juke Box Jury

435. In 1964, Johnny Kidd and the Pirates released an album featuring the hit single "I'll Never Get Over You." What is the title of this album?
a) "The Pirates Are Back"
b) "Ship of Dreams"
c) "Always and Ever"
d) "So What"

436. Which guitarist was a member of Johnny Kidd and the Pirates and later joined the influential British rock band The Pirates, featuring Mick Green on guitar?
a) Ritchie Blackmore
b) Eric Clapton
c) Mick Taylor

d) Johnny Spence

Johnny Kidd & The Pirates (Answers Page 111)

437. Johnny Kidd and the Pirates are often associated with a
distinctive eyepatch worn by Johnny Kidd. What was the
reason for the eyepatch?
a) Fashion statement
b) Pirate-themed persona
c) Stage persona inspired by a film character
d) Injury sustained in a car accident

438. Tragically, Johnny Kidd passed away in 1966 at the age of
27. What was the cause of his untimely death?
a) Drug overdose
b) Plane crash
c) Car accident
d) Illness

King Crimson (Answers Page 111)

439. Who was the founding member and guitarist of King
Crimson?
a) Greg Lake
b) Robert Fripp
c) Bill Bruford
d) John Wetton

440. Which year did King Crimson release their groundbreaking
debut album, "In the Court of the Crimson King"?
a) 1967
b) 1969
c) 1971
d) 1973

441. What instrument did Ian McDonald primarily play in King
Crimson?
a) Guitar
b) Bass
c) Keyboards
d) Saxophone

King Crimson (Answers Page 111)

442. Which of the following albums marked the return of King Crimson after a hiatus in the 1970s?
a) "Larks' Tongues in Aspic"
b) "Red"
c) "Discipline"
d) "In the Wake of Poseidon"

443. In addition to being a guitarist, Robert Fripp is known for his proficiency on which instrument?
a) Violin
b) Flute
c) Mellotron
d) Chapman Stick

444. Who replaced Greg Lake in King Crimson?
a) John Wetton
b) Adrian Belew
c) Tony Levin
d) Gordon Haskell

445. Which King Crimson album features the track "21st Century Schizoid Man"?
a) "In the Court of the Crimson King"
b) "Lizard"
c) "Starless and Bible Black"
d) "Islands"

446. What is the title of the instrumental track that opens the "Larks' Tongues in Aspic" album?
a) "Starless"
b) "Fracture"
c) "Larks' Tongues in Aspic, Part One"
d) "The ConstruKction of Light"

447. Which drummer was a member of King Crimson and later played with bands like Genesis and Yes?
a) Carl Palmer

b) Bill Bruford
c) Phil Collins
d) Alan White

King Crimson (Answers Page 111)

448. King Crimson's 1973 album "Larks' Tongues in Aspic" marked the inclusion of which instrument in the lineup?
a) Violin
b) Flute
c) Vibraphone
d) Mellotron

449. What term is often used to describe King Crimson's approach to music, characterized by intricate compositions and unconventional time signatures?
a) Glam rock
b) Prog rock
c) Punk rock
d) Blues rock

Jonathan King (Answers Page 111)

450. Jonathan King, a British singer, songwriter, and producer, had a hit in 1965 with a song that reached number three on the UK Singles Chart. What is the title of this hit single?
a) "Everyone's Gone to the Moon"
b) "A World of Our Own"
c) "Shakin' All Over"
d) "Bus Stop"

451. In addition to his musical career, Jonathan King is known for his work as a record producer. Which famous British rock band did he produce during the early 1970s?
a) The Rolling Stones
b) The Beatles
c) Genesis
d) The Who

452. Jonathan King released an album in 1969 that featured a controversial cover and title, reflecting his sense of humor. What is the title of this album?
a) "Laughing All the Way to the Bank"

b) "Everyone's Gone to the Moon"
c) "The Banned Album"
d) "Jonathan King Sings"

Jonathan King (Answers Page 111)

453. What is the name of Jonathan King's record label, which he founded in the 1960s and played a significant role in the British music scene?
a) Apple Records
b) Decca Records
c) UK Records
d) Island Records

454. Jonathan King wrote and produced a hit single for a British singer in the 1960s, but the song became even more famous when covered by a Swedish group. What is the song?
a) "She's Not There"
b) "He's in Town"
c) "It's Good News Week"
d) "Summer Holiday"

Johnny Kidd & The Pirates (Answers)

432. b) Johnny Kidd
433. a) "Shakin' All Over"
434. b) Top of the Pops
435. a) "The Pirates Are Back"
436. a) Ritchie Blackmore
437. d) Injury sustained in a car accident
438. b) Plane crash

King Crimson (Answers)

439. b) Robert Fripp
440. b) 1969
441. c) Keyboards
442. c) "Discipline"
443. d) Chapman Stick
444. a) John Wetton
445. a) "In the Court of the Crimson King"
446. c) "Larks' Tongues in Aspic, Part One"
447. b) Bill Bruford
448. a) Violin
449. b) Prog rock

Jonathan King (Answers)

450. a) "Everyone's Gone to the Moon"
451. c) Genesis
452. c) "The Banned Album"
453. c) UK Records
454. b) "He's in Town"

The Kinks (Answers Page 118)

455. Who are the primary founding members of The Kinks?
    a) Ray and Dave Davies
    b) Mick Jagger and Keith Richards
    c) John Lennon and Paul McCartney
    d) Roger Daltrey and Pete Townshend

456. The Kinks' breakthrough single "You Really Got Me" was released in which year?
    a) 1962
    b) 1964
    c) 1966
    d) 1968

457. What is the title of The Kinks' concept album released in 1968, featuring a village green theme?
    a) "Face to Face"
    b) "Arthur (Or the Decline and Fall of the British Empire)"
    c) "Something Else by The Kinks"
    d) "The Kinks Are The Village Green Preservation Society"

458. Which hit song by The Kinks satirizes the mod subculture and was released in 1966?
    a) "All Day and All of the Night"
    b) "Waterloo Sunset"
    c) "Dedicated Follower of Fashion"
    d) "Sunny Afternoon"

459. What character did Ray Davies portray in the rock opera "Preservation: Act 1" released in 1973?
    a) Mr. Black
    b) Lola
    c) Victoria
    d) Johnny Thunder

The Kinks (Answers Page 118)

460. The Kinks' album "Lola Versus Powerman and the Moneygoround, Part One" includes a song about the music industry. What is the title of this track?
a) "Lola"
b) "Celluloid Heroes"
c) "Apeman"
d) "Top of the Pops"

461. Who served as the primary songwriter for The Kinks?
a) Ray Davies
b) Dave Davies
c) Pete Quaife
d) Mick Avory

462. The Kinks' album "Muswell Hillbillies" explores themes related to urban life. In which year was it released?
a) 1970
b) 1972
c) 1974
d) 1976

463. What is the title of The Kinks' hit single released in 1967 that tells the story of a lazy afternoon?
a) "Waterloo Sunset"
b) "Sunny Afternoon"
c) "Dead End Street"
d) "Victoria"

464. Which album marked The Kinks' return to commercial success in the 1980s with hits like "Come Dancing"?
a) "Sleepwalker"
b) "Low Budget"
c) "Give the People What They Want"
d) "State of Confusion"

The Kinks (Answers Page 118)

465. What is the title of The Kinks' rock opera released in 1975
     that explores the story of a fictional rock band?
     a) "Lola Versus Powerman and the Moneygoround, Part
     One"
     b) "Preservation: Act 1"
     c) "Soap Opera"
     d) "Schoolboys in Disgrace"

466. The Kinks' song "Waterloo Sunset" is often regarded as one
     of their greatest. What is the name of the character
     mentioned in the lyrics?
     a) Terry
     b) Julie
     c) Lola
     d) Arthur

The Koobas (Answers Page 118)

467. Who was the lead vocalist and guitarist of The Koobas?
     a) Roy Orbison
     b) Stuart Leathwood
     c) Keith Ellis
     d) Tony O'Riley

468. The Koobas gained recognition for their association with
     which iconic British rock band, for whom they served as a
     backing band in the mid-1960s?
     a) The Rolling Stones
     b) The Beatles
     c) The Kinks
     d) The Who

469. In 1965, The Koobas released a single titled:
     a) "Hey Joe"
     b) "Taxman"
     c) "Sweet Little Sixteen"
     d) "Take Me For A Little While"

The Koobas (Answers Page 118)

470. The Koobas' music is often associated with which musical
genre?
a) Psychedelic rock
b) Blues rock
c) Folk rock
d) Merseybeat

471. What was the title of The Koobas' debut album, released in
1969?
a) "The Koobas"
b) "Barricades"
c) "Sgt. Kooba's Lonely Hearts Club Band"
d) "Magic Potion"

Billy J. Kramer (And The Dakotas) (Answers Page 118)

472. What was the role of The Dakotas in relation to the famous
British rock artist they were associated with in the 1960s?
a) Backup band
b) Songwriting duo
c) Opening act
d) Manager

473. In 1963, The Dakotas and Billy J. Kramer had a hit with a
song written by John Lennon and Paul McCartney. What is
the title of this song?
a) "Twist and Shout"
b) "I Want to Hold Your Hand"
c) "Bad to Me"
d) "She Loves You"

474. What instrument did Bruce Johnston, a member of The
Dakotas, play in the band?
a) Guitar
b) Drums
c) Bass
d) Keyboard

Billy J. Kramer (And The Dakotas) (Answers Page 118)

475. After their collaboration with Billy J. Kramer, The Dakotas
continued to work with other artists. Who was the Scottish
singer they backed in the late 1960s?
a) Donovan
b) Lulu
c) Sandie Shaw
d) Petula Clark

476. What was the original name of The Dakotas before they
became associated with Billy J. Kramer?
a) The Crescents
b) The Shadows
c) The Dreamers
d) The Silver Beetles

477. The Dakotas' instrumental track "The Cruel Sea" became a
hit in 1963. Which genre is most closely associated with this
song?
a) Surf rock
b) Psychedelic rock
c) Rockabilly
d) Blues rock

478. What was the title of the debut album released by Billy J.
Kramer with The Dakotas in 1963?
a) "Little Children"
b) "Listen..."
c) "I'll Keep You Satisfied"
d) "Trains and Boats and Planes"

479. The Dakotas had a successful career in the 1960s, and their
association with Billy J. Kramer resulted in several chart-
topping hits. Which city did the band originate from?
a) Manchester
b) Liverpool
c) London
d) Birmingham

Billy J. Kramer (And The Dakotas) (Answers Page 118)

480. What was the birth name of the lead singer Billy J. Kramer?
a) William Howard Ashton
b) John Winston Lennon
c) Paul McCartney
d) Richard Starkey

481. Billy J. Kramer's biggest hit, "Little Children," was released in 1964. Who wrote this song?
a) Mick Jagger and Keith Richards
b) Pete Townshend
c) Gerry Goffin and Carole King
d) John Lennon and Paul McCartney

482. Which American record producer played a crucial role in the early success of Billy J. Kramer and The Dakotas by signing them to Capitol Records?
a) Phil Spector
b) Brian Wilson
c) Quincy Jones
d) Berry Gordy

483. Billy J. Kramer and The Dakotas had several Top 10 hits. Which one of the following songs was not a hit for the band?
a) "Do You Want to Know a Secret"
b) "I'll Keep You Satisfied"
c) "Bad to Me"
d) "She's a Woman"

484. What instrument did Billy J. Kramer play in the band?
a) Guitar
b) Bass
c) Keyboard
d) None – he was the lead vocalist

485. Which famous Beatles song did Billy J. Kramer and The Dakotas cover and release as a single in 1964?
a) "A Hard Day's Night"
b) "Can't Buy Me Love"

c) "I Should Have Known Better"
d) "From Me to You"

The Kinks (Answers)

455. a) Ray and Dave Davies
456. b) 1964
457. d) "The Kinks Are The Village Green Preservation Society"
458. c) "Dedicated Follower of Fashion"
459. a) Mr. Black
460. d) "Top of the Pops"
461. a) Ray Davies
462. a) 1970
463. b) "Sunny Afternoon"
464. c) "Give the People What They Want"
465. c) "Soap Opera"
466. b) Julie

The Koobas (Answers)

467. b) Stuart Leathwood
468. b) The Beatles
469. d) "Take Me For A Little While"
470. d) Merseybeat
471. b) "Barricades"

Billy J. Kramer (And The Dakotas) (Answers)

472. a) Backup band
473. c) "Bad to Me"
474. d) Keyboard
475. b) Lulu
476. a) The Crescents
477. a) Surf rock
478. b) "Listen..."
479. a) Manchester
480. a) William Howard Ashton
481. c) Gerry Goffin and Carole King
482. a) Phil Spector
483. a) "Do You Want to Know a Secret"
484. d) None – he was the lead vocalist

485. c) "I Should Have Known Better"

Led Zeppelin (Answers Page 125)

486. Who was the lead guitarist and primary songwriter for Led
Zeppelin?
a) Jimmy Page
b) Robert Plant
c) John Bonham
d) John Paul Jones

487. When did Led Zeppelin release their self-titled debut album?
a) 1967
b) 1968
c) 1969
d) 1970

488. What iconic rock song opens Led Zeppelin's fourth album
and is often associated with the band's live performances?
a) "Whole Lotta Love"
b) "Stairway to Heaven"
c) "Black Dog"
d) "Rock and Roll"

489. Which member of Led Zeppelin played bass guitar and
keyboard for the band?
a) John Bonham
b) Jimmy Page
c) Robert Plant
d) John Paul Jones

490. Led Zeppelin's second album features a mix of blues and
hard rock. What is the title of this album?
a) "Led Zeppelin III"
b) "Led Zeppelin II"
c) "Led Zeppelin IV"
d) "Physical Graffiti"

491. What was the name of Led Zeppelin's record label, founded
by the band in 1974?
a) Swan Song Records
b) Atlantic Records

c) Epic Records
d) Mercury Records

Led Zeppelin (Answers Page 125)

492. Which Led Zeppelin song is often considered one of the
greatest guitar solos of all time and showcases Jimmy Page's
exceptional guitar work?
a) "Dazed and Confused"
b) "Heartbreaker"
c) "Black Dog"
d) "Stairway to Heaven"

493. Led Zeppelin's untitled fourth album is commonly known
by what other name?
a) "Led Zeppelin II"
b) "Houses of the Holy"
c) "Physical Graffiti"
d) "Led Zeppelin IV"

494. Which Led Zeppelin song features lyrics inspired by J.R.R.
Tolkien's "The Lord of the Rings"?
a) "The Battle of Evermore"
b) "Kashmir"
c) "Ramble On"
d) "Misty Mountain Hop"

495. Led Zeppelin disbanded after the death of which member in
1980?
a) Jimmy Page
b) Robert Plant
c) John Bonham
d) John Paul Jones

496. Led Zeppelin's live album "The Song Remains the Same"
was recorded during a series of concerts in which city?
a) London
b) New York
c) Los Angeles
d) Tokyo

The Liverbirds (Answers Page 125)

497. Who was the lead vocalist and guitarist of The Liverbirds?
    a) Sheila McGlory
    b) Mary McGlory
    c) Sylvia Saunders
    d) Pam Birch

498. The Liverbirds originated from which British city?
    a) Liverpool
    b) Manchester
    c) London
    d) Birmingham

499. The Liverbirds gained popularity in the 1960s with their
    energetic performances and were often compared to which
    iconic male rock band?
    a) The Rolling Stones
    b) The Beatles
    c) The Who
    d) The Kinks

500. What was the title of The Liverbirds' debut single, released
    in 1964?
    a) "Peanut Butter"
    b) "Why Do You Hang Around Me?"
    c) "Diddley Daddy"
    d) "He's Something Else"

501. The Liverbirds were known for covering songs by which
    American rhythm and blues artist?
    a) Chuck Berry
    b) Little Richard
    c) Bo Diddley
    d) Fats Domino

Love Affair (Answers Page 125)

502. What was Love Affair's biggest hit single, released in 1968, that reached the top of the UK Singles Chart?
a) "Everlasting Love"
b) "Rainbow Valley"
c) "Bringing on Back the Good Times"
d) "A Day Without Love"

503. Who was the lead singer of Love Affair known for his distinctive soulful voice?
a) Steve Ellis
b) Mick Jackson
c) Ken Andrew
d) Rex Brayley

504. Love Affair released their debut album in 1968. What was the title of this album?
a) "No Strings Attached"
b) "Love Affair"
c) "Everlasting Love"
d) "Bringing on Back the Good Times"

505. Prior to becoming Love Affair, the band was known by a different name. What was that original name?
a) The Paramounts
b) The Soul Survivors
c) The Teenbeats
d) The Cavaliers

506. Love Affair had success covering the song "Rainbow Valley." Who originally recorded this song?
a) The Tremeloes
b) The Beatles
c) The Move
d) The Easybeats

Manfred Mann (Answers Page 125)

507. Who was the eponymous keyboardist and leader of Manfred
Mann?
a) Mick Jagger
b) Manfred Mann
c) Eric Clapton
d) Van Morrison

508. Manfred Mann's cover of Bob Dylan's song "The Mighty
Quinn (Quinn the Eskimo)" became a hit in which year?
a) 1964
b) 1967
c) 1969
d) 1972

509. What was the original name of Manfred Mann's band before
they adopted the name "Manfred Mann"?
a) The Animals
b) The Yardbirds
c) The Mann-Hugg Blues Brothers
d) The Hollies

510. Which Manfred Mann song features the famous refrain
"Doo Wah Diddy Diddy"?
a) "Pretty Flamingo"
b) "Do Wah Diddy Diddy"
c) "Sha La La"
d) "Mighty Quinn (Quinn the Eskimo)"

511. Manfred Mann's Earth Band, a later incarnation of the band,
gained success in the 1970s. What was their hit cover of a
Bruce Springsteen song?
a) "Blinded by the Light"
b) "Spirit in the Night"
c) "Born to Run"
d) "Thunder Road"

Manfred Mann (Answers Page 125)

512. What was the title of Manfred Mann's debut studio album, released in 1964?
a) "The Five Faces of Manfred Mann"
b) "Mann Made"
c) "Pretty Flamingo"
d) "The Manfred Mann Album"

513. Which member of Manfred Mann wrote the band's 1969 hit single "Fox on the Run"?
a) Manfred Mann
b) Mike Hugg
c) Paul Jones
d) Mike d'Abo

514. What was the title of Manfred Mann's 1968 concept album, which featured jazz and experimental elements?
a) "Mann Made"
b) "Up the Junction"
c) "The Mighty Quinn"
d) "The Ascent of Mann"

515. What was the last studio album released by Manfred Mann with the original lineup in the 1960s?
a) "Mann Made"
b) "Up the Junction"
c) "The Mighty Quinn"
d) "Mighty Garvey!"

Led Zeppelin (Answers)

486. a) Jimmy Page
487. c) 1969
488. a) "Whole Lotta Love"
489. d) John Paul Jones
490. b) "Led Zeppelin II"
491. a) Swan Song Records
492. b) "Heartbreaker"
493. d) "Led Zeppelin IV"
494. a) "The Battle of Evermore"
495. c) John Bonham
496. b) New York

The Liverbirds (Answers)

497. a) Sheila McGlory
498. a) Liverpool
499. b) The Beatles
500. b) "Why Do You Hang Around Me?"
501. c) Bo Diddley

Love Affair (Answers)

502. a) "Everlasting Love"
503. a) Steve Ellis
504. b) "Love Affair"
505. c) The Soul Survivors
506. d) The Easybeats

Manfred Mann (Answers)

507. b) Manfred Mann
508. c) 1969
509. c) The Mann-Hugg Blues Brothers
510. b) "Do Wah Diddy Diddy"
511. a) "Blinded by the Light"
512. a) "The Five Faces of Manfred Mann"
513. b) Mike Hugg
514. c) "The Ascent of Mann"

515. d) "Mighty Garvey!"

John Mayall (& The Bluesbreakers)
(Answers Page 132)

516. Who is often referred to as the "Godfather of British Blues"
and is known for leading the influential 1960s British rock
band John Mayall & the Bluesbreakers?
a) Eric Clapton
b) John Mayall
c) Mick Jagger
d) Jimmy Page

517. Which legendary guitarist first gained widespread
recognition as a member of John Mayall & the Bluesbreakers
before joining Cream and later forming Derek and the
Dominos?
a) Jimi Hendrix
b) Jeff Beck
c) Peter Green
d) Eric Clapton

518. John Mayall's album "Blues Breakers with Eric Clapton,"
released in 1966, is often referred to as the "Beano Album."
Why is it called the "Beano Album"?
a) Clapton's nickname was Beano
b) Mayall's nickname was Beano
c) The album cover features the Beano comic
d) It was recorded at Beano Studios

519. In addition to Eric Clapton, which guitarist, known for his
work with Fleetwood Mac, was a member of John Mayall &
the Bluesbreakers during the late 1960s?
a) Peter Green
b) Mick Taylor
c) Jeff Beck
d) Jimmy Page

520. John Mayall & the Bluesbreakers' 1968 album "Bare Wires"
marked a departure from traditional blues, incorporating
elements of which genre?
a) Psychedelic Rock
b) Jazz Fusion
c) Country

d) Folk

John Mayall (& The Bluesbreakers)
(Answers Page 132)

521. Who played bass guitar for John Mayall & the Bluesbreakers
and later went on to join Fleetwood Mac as the band's co-
founder?
a) John McVie
b) Jack Bruce
c) John Paul Jones
d) Chris Squire

522. Which instrument did John Mayall primarily play himself in
the Bluesbreakers during the 1960s?
a) Guitar
b) Harmonica
c) Piano
d) Saxophone

The Merseybeats (Answers Page 132)

523. What was the debut single released by the Merseybeats in
1963 that reached the Top 10 in the UK Singles Chart?
a) "Wishin' and Hopin'"
b) "I Think of You"
c) "Don't Let It Happen to Us"
d) "Sorrow"

524. Which member of the Merseybeats later became a member
of the band The Fourmost?
a) Tony Crane
b) Billy Kinsley
c) Dave Goldberg
d) John Banks

525. In 1964, the Merseybeats released a cover of a classic song
that became one of their biggest hits. What was the title of
this single?
a) "I'll Keep You Satisfied"
b) "It's Love That Really Counts"
c) "Penny Lane"
d) "You're My World"

The Merseybeats (Answers Page 132)

526. What was the name of the Merseybeats' first studio album, released in 1964?
a) "Beat & Ballads"
b) "The Merseybeats"
c) "I Stand Accused"
d) "On Stage"

527. Which Merseybeats song, released in 1965, was later covered by The Searchers and became a hit for both bands?
a) "I Stand Accused"
b) "Wishin' and Hopin'"
c) "It's Love That Really Counts"
d) "Milkman"

528. The Merseybeats were part of the British Invasion and performed in the United States on the same Ed Sullivan Show episode as which other famous British band?
a) The Rolling Stones
b) The Beatles
c) The Kinks
d) The Dave Clark Five

529. What was the final single released by the Merseybeats before their initial breakup in 1966?
a) "Don't Turn Around"
b) "Really Mystified"
c) "I Think of You"
d) "Last Night"

The Mindbenders (Answers Page 132)

530. What was the Mindbenders' first major hit single, released in 1966?
a) "A Groovy Kind of Love"
b) "Game of Love"
c) "Can't Live with You (Can't Live Without You)"
d) "Ashes to Ashes"

The Mindbenders (Answers Page 132)

531. Before becoming the Mindbenders, the band was originally known by a different name. What was that name?
a) The Tremeloes
b) The Mockingbirds
c) The Yardbirds
d) The Zombies

532. Which member of the Mindbenders later achieved success as a solo artist with the hit "A Groovy Kind of Love"?
a) Eric Stewart
b) Graham Gouldman
c) Bob Lang
d) Ric Rothwell

533. In 1966, the Mindbenders released an album containing their hit single "Game of Love." What was the title of this album?
a) "Mindbending Sounds"
b) "With Woman in Mind"
c) "A Groovy Kind of Love"
d) "Game of Love"

534. Which famous filmmaker directed the Mindbenders' performance scenes in the 1967 film "To Sir, with Love"?
a) Stanley Kubrick
b) Alfred Hitchcock
c) Sidney Lumet
d) James Clavell

535. What was the Mindbenders' second highest-charting single in the UK, released in 1966?
a) "Um, Um, Um, Um, Um, Um"
b) "It's Getting Harder All the Time"
c) "Ashes to Ashes"
d) "Off and Running"

The Mindbenders (Answers Page 132)

536. The Mindbenders briefly served as the backing band for which female singer before she pursued a successful solo career?
a) Lulu
b) Dusty Springfield
c) Petula Clark
d) Sandie Shaw

The Mojos (Answers Page 132)

537. Who was the lead vocalist and frontman of The Mojos?
a) Paul McCartney
b) Adrian Barber
c) Stu James
d) Lewis Collins

538. The Mojos achieved chart success with their hit single:
a) "Twist and Shout"
b) "Bad to Me"
c) "Do You Love Me"
d) "She Loves You"

539. In addition to their original songs, The Mojos were known for covering tracks by which American R&B artist?
a) Chuck Berry
b) Little Richard
c) Bo Diddley
d) Ray Charles

540. The Mojos hailed from which English city known for its vibrant music scene during the 1960s?
a) Liverpool
b) Manchester
c) London
d) Birmingham

The Mojos (Answers Page 132)

541. The Mojos' lineup underwent changes during their career. Which member later became a successful record producer, working with artists like Elton John and The Bee Gees?
a) Lewis Collins
b) Adrian Barber
c) Nicky Crouch
d) Aynsley Dunbar

John Mayall (& The Bluesbreakers) (Answers)

516. b) John Mayall
517. d) Eric Clapton
518. c) The album cover features the Beano comic
519. a) Peter Green
520. a) Psychedelic Rock
521. a) John McVie
522. b) Harmonica

The Merseybeats (Answers)

523. c) "Don't Let It Happen to Us"
524. b) Billy Kinsley
525. a) "I'll Keep You Satisfied"
526. b) "The Merseybeats"
527. c) "It's Love That Really Counts"
528. b) The Beatles
529. a) "Don't Turn Around"

The Mindbenders (Answers)

530. b) "Game of Love"
531. b) The Mockingbirds
532. a) Eric Stewart
533. b) "With Woman in Mind"
534. a) Stanley Kubrick
535. a) "Ashes to Ashes"
536. b) Dusty Springfield

The Mojos (Answers)

537. c) Stu James
538. b) "Bad to Me"
539. b) Little Richard
540. a) Liverpool
541. b) Adrian Barber

The Montanas (Answers Page 139)

542. What was the debut single released by The Montanas in 1965?
    a) "Ciao Baby"
    b) "Difference of Opinion"
    c) "You've Got to Be Loved"
    d) "Let's Get a Little Sentimental"

543. The Montanas' biggest hit, released in 1967, was titled:
    a) "That's When Happiness Began"
    b) "Ciao Baby"
    c) "You've Got to Be Loved"
    d) "Let's Get a Little Sentimental"

544. What genre of music is The Montanas most commonly associated with?
    a) Psychedelic rock
    b) Blues rock
    c) Progressive rock
    d) Folk rock

545. Which Montanas' single features a cover of a classic Bob Dylan song?
    a) "Ciao Baby"
    b) "The World Is a Circle"
    c) "Difference of Opinion"
    d) "You've Got to Be Loved"

546. The Montanas' lineup included lead singer Graham Foote. What instrument did Graham Foote play in the band?
    a) Guitar
    b) Bass
    c) Drums
    d) Keyboard

The Moody Blues (Answers Page 139)

547. What was the Moody Blues' first UK hit single, released in 1964?
   a) "Nights in White Satin"
   b) "Go Now!"
   c) "Tuesday Afternoon"
   d) "Ride My See-Saw"

548. The Moody Blues are known for pioneering a unique fusion of rock and classical music. Which album marked their transition to this style in the late 1960s?
   a) "Days of Future Passed"
   b) "In Search of the Lost Chord"
   c) "To Our Children's Children's Children"
   d) "On the Threshold of a Dream"

549. Who was the original lead singer of the Moody Blues during the recording of "Go Now!"?
   a) Justin Hayward
   b) Ray Thomas
   c) Denny Laine
   d) Mike Pinder

550. Which member of the Moody Blues is credited with writing the majority of the band's lyrics?
   a) Justin Hayward
   b) Ray Thomas
   c) John Lodge
   d) Graeme Edge

551. The Moody Blues' concept album "In Search of the Lost Chord" (1968) featured a distinctive instrument associated with the band. What was it?
   a) Flute
   b) Mellotron
   c) Sitar
   d) Theremin

The Moody Blues (Answers Page 139)

552. Which Moody Blues album, released in 1969, included the
hit singles "Question" and "The Story in Your Eyes"?
a) "To Our Children's Children's Children"
b) "On the Threshold of a Dream"
c) "A Question of Balance"
d) "Seventh Sojourn"

553. The Moody Blues are known for their philosophical and
introspective lyrics. Which member of the band was a
principal lyricist and played the flute?
a) Justin Hayward
b) Ray Thomas
c) Mike Pinder
d) John Lodge

554. What was the Moody Blues' first album to feature Justin
Hayward and John Lodge as permanent members?
a) "Days of Future Passed"
b) "On the Threshold of a Dream"
c) "In Search of the Lost Chord"
d) "To Our Children's Children's Children"

555. The Moody Blues were inducted into the Rock and Roll Hall
of Fame in 2018. Which classic Moody Blues album was
released in 1972?
a) "Seventh Sojourn"
b) "Long Distance Voyager"
c) "Every Good Boy Deserves Favour"
d) "Octave"

556. Which Moody Blues album, released in 1970, is a thematic
exploration of the moon landing and space travel?
a) "A Question of Balance"
b) "Seventh Sojourn"
c) "To Our Children's Children's Children"
d) "On the Threshold of a Dream"

The Moontrekkers (Answers Page 139)

557. What was the instrumental hit single released by the
Moontrekkers in 1962 that reached the UK Top 50?
a) "Telstar"
b) "Pipeline"
c) "Night of the Vampire"
d) "Hatashiai"

558. The Moontrekkers were known for incorporating
unconventional instruments into their music. What
instrument was prominently featured in their hit "Night of
the Vampire"?
a) Theremin
b) Sitar
c) Dulcimer
d) Bagpipes

559. Who was the record producer behind the Moontrekkers' hit
"Night of the Vampire"?
a) Joe Meek
b) George Martin
c) Phil Spector
d) Mickie Most

560. In addition to "Night of the Vampire," the Moontrekkers
released another instrumental single in 1963. What was its
title?
a) "Siboney"
b) "The Bogey Man"
c) "Geronimo"
d) "Zambesi"

561. What was the name of the Moontrekkers' only studio album,
released in 1963?
a) "Siboney"
b) "The Moontrekkers"
c) "Lost Planet"
d) "Surfin' Safari"

The Moontrekkers (Answers Page 139)

562. Which of the following films featured the Moontrekkers'
     music on its soundtrack?
     a) "A Hard Day's Night"
     b) "The Good, the Bad and the Ugly"
     c) "Goldfinger"
     d) "Psycho"

563. The Moontrekkers' music is often associated with which
     musical genre?
     a) Surf rock
     b) Psychedelic rock
     c) British Invasion
     d) Merseybeat

564. What was the B-side of the Moontrekkers' single "Night of
     the Vampire"?
     a) "Melodie D'Amour"
     b) "There's Something at the Bottom of the Well"
     c) "Siboney"
     d) "Love Walked In"

Mott The Hoople (Answers Page 139)

565. What was the original name of Mott the Hoople before they
     adopted their famous moniker?
     a) The Soul Patches
     b) The Silence
     c) The Vagabonds
     d) The Glitter Boys

566. Mott the Hoople's breakthrough single, released in 1972,
     was a cover of which David Bowie song?
     a) "Space Oddity"
     b) "Heroes"
     c) "Starman"
     d) "All the Young Dudes"

Mott The Hoople (Answers Page 139)

567. The lead singer of Mott the Hoople, who later embarked on
a solo career, is:
a) Ian Hunter
b) Mick Ralphs
c) Verden Allen
d) Overend Watts

568. What was the title of Mott the Hoople's 1973 album
produced by David Bowie, which included the hit single "All
the Young Dudes"?
a) "Mott"
b) "Mad Shadows"
c) "Brain Capers"
d) "All the Way from Memphis"

569. Mott the Hoople announced their temporary disbandment
in 1974 but later reformed. What was the name of their 1974
farewell tour?
a) The Last Hurrah
b) Mott's Final Stand
c) Hoople's Goodbye
d) The Farewell Fling

The Montanas (Answers)

542. b) "Difference of Opinion"
543. c) "You've Got to Be Loved"
544. a) Psychedelic rock
545. b) "The World Is a Circle"
546. a) Guitar

The Moody Blues (Answers)

547. b) "Go Now!"
548. a) "Days of Future Passed"
549. c) Denny Laine
550. d) Graeme Edge
551. b) Mellotron
552. c) "A Question of Balance"
553. b) Ray Thomas
554. b) "On the Threshold of a Dream"
555. a) "Seventh Sojourn"
556. c) "To Our Children's Children's Children"

The Moontrekkers (Answers)

557. c) "Night of the Vampire"
558. a) Theremin
559. a) Joe Meek
560. b) "The Bogey Man"
561. c) "Lost Planet"
562. c) "Goldfinger"
563. a) Surf rock
564. b) "There's Something at the Bottom of the Well"

Mott The Hoople (Answers)

565. c) The Vagabonds
566. d) "All the Young Dudes"
567. a) Ian Hunter
568. a) "Mott"
569. c) Hoople's Goodbye

The Move (Answers Page 146)

570. Who was the founder and lead vocalist of the 1960s British
     rock band The Move?
     a) Roy Wood
     b) Jeff Lynne
     c) Bev Bevan
     d) Carl Wayne

571. The Move's debut single, released in 1966, became a chart-
     topping hit in the UK. What is the title of this iconic song?
     a) "Flowers in the Rain"
     b) "Fire Brigade"
     c) "I Can Hear the Grass Grow"
     d) "Blackberry Way"

572. In 1968, The Move released an ambitious album that
     included a suite of interconnected songs. What is the title of
     this progressive rock masterpiece?
     a) "Message from the Country"
     b) "Shazam"
     c) "Looking On"
     d) "ELO 2"

573. Before forming Electric Light Orchestra (ELO), both Jeff
     Lynne and Bev Bevan were members of which influential
     band alongside their time in The Move?
     a) The Moody Blues
     b) The Hollies
     c) The Idle Race
     d) The Spencer Davis Group

574. The Move was known for its energetic live performances
     and unconventional stage antics. What memorable prop did
     the band incorporate into their stage show?
     a) A giant flower
     b) A psychedelic light show
     c) A wrecking ball
     d) A rotating drum riser

The Move (Answers Page 146)

575. What was the title of The Move's 1967 debut album, which
featured hits like "Night of Fear" and "I Can Hear the Grass
Grow"?
a) "The Move"
b) "Shazam"
c) "Looking On"
d) "Something Else from The Move"

576. Which member of The Move later played a significant role
in the formation of the Electric Light Orchestra (ELO)?
a) Roy Wood
b) Jeff Lynne
c) Bev Bevan
d) Carl Wayne

577. The Move's song "Blackberry Way" reached the number one
spot on the UK Singles Chart in 1968. What was the theme
of the song's lyrics?
a) Love and Romance
b) Anti-war protest
c) Nostalgia for the past
d) Social injustice

578. In the late 1960s, The Move collaborated with the British
comedian Roy Wood on a novelty song that became a festive
hit. What is the title of this Christmas single?
a) "California Man"
b) "Fire Brigade"
c) "Blackberry Way"
d) "I Wish It Could Be Christmas Every Day"

579. What was the reason behind Carl Wayne's departure from
The Move in 1970?
a) Pursuit of a solo career
b) Creative differences
c) Health issues
d) Joining another band

The Move (Answers Page 146)

580. The Move's lineup included musicians who later became part of the supergroup Traveling Wilburys. Which member was part of both The Move and the Traveling Wilburys?
a) Roy Wood
b) Jeff Lynne
c) Bev Bevan
d) Carl Wayne

581. In 2007, The Move received a recognition honor at the UK Music Hall of Fame. What was the title of the documentary film that chronicled the history of the band and its impact on British music?
a) "Looking On"
b) "California Man"
c) "The Move Chronicles"
d) "Flowers in the Rain"

The Nashville Teens (Answers Page 146)

582. What was the Nashville Teens' biggest hit single, released in 1964?
a) "Wishing"
b) "Google Eye"
c) "Tobacco Road"
d) "Find My Way Back Home"

583. The Nashville Teens gained popularity for their energetic performances. What city in the United States inspired the title of their hit single "Tobacco Road"?
a) Memphis
b) Nashville
c) Atlanta
d) Durham

584. Which member of the Nashville Teens wrote the lyrics for their hit single "Tobacco Road"?
a) Ray Phillips
b) Arthur Sharp
c) Mick Dunford
d) John Allen

The Nashville Teens (Answers Page 146)

585. In addition to "Tobacco Road," the Nashville Teens had another hit single in 1964. What was its title?
a) "Google Eye"
b) "Wagon Wheel"
c) "Find My Way Back Home"
d) "The Little Bird"

586. Which American singer originally recorded the song "Tobacco Road," which later became a hit for the Nashville Teens?
a) Lou Rawls
b) John D. Loudermilk
c) Jim Ford
d) J.D. Sumner

587. The Nashville Teens were associated with which musical genre during the 1960s?
a) Psychedelic rock
b) Merseybeat
c) Skiffle
d) Rhythm and Blues

588. Which Rolling Stones song did the Nashville Teens cover and release as a single in 1965?
a) "Paint It, Black"
b) "Jumpin' Jack Flash"
c) "Like a Rolling Stone"
d) "The Last Time"

589. What was the name of the Nashville Teens' debut studio album, released in 1964?
a) "Tobacco Road"
b) "Find My Way Back Home"
c) "The Nashville Teens"
d) "Wagon Wheel"

Nazareth (Answers Page 146)

590. What was Nazareth's debut album, released in 1971?
   a) "Hair of the Dog"
   b) "Rampant"
   c) "Exercises"
   d) "Nazareth"

591. Nazareth's most well-known album, featuring the hit song "Love Hurts," was released in which year?
   a) 1973
   b) 1975
   c) 1977
   d) 1980

592. Which member of Nazareth served as the lead vocalist and joined the band in the early 1970s?
   a) Pete Agnew
   b) Manny Charlton
   c) Dan McCafferty
   d) Darrell Sweet

593. Nazareth's cover of which Joni Mitchell song became a hit single for the band?
   a) "Big Yellow Taxi"
   b) "Woodstock"
   c) "A Case of You"
   d) "This Flight Tonight"

594. What was the name of Nazareth's 1977 album that featured the hit single "Love Hurts"?
   a) "Expect No Mercy"
   b) "Play 'n' the Game"
   c) "Close Enough for Rock 'n' Roll"
   d) "Hair of the Dog"

595. Which rock anthem by Nazareth became a fan favorite and is often performed in their live shows?
   a) "Bad Bad Boy"
   b) "Love Leads to Madness"
   c) "Dream On"
   d) "Razamanaz"

Nazareth (Answers Page 146)

596. Nazareth's song "Holy Roller" is from which album,
released in 1975?
a) "Expect No Mercy"
b) "Hair of the Dog"
c) "Close Enough for Rock 'n' Roll"
d) "Razamanaz"

The Move (Answers)

570. a) Roy Wood
571. a) "Flowers in the Rain"
572. c) "Looking On"
573. c) The Idle Race
574. c) A wrecking ball
575. a) "The Move"
576. b) Jeff Lynne
577. c) Nostalgia for the past
578. d) "I Wish It Could Be Christmas Every Day"
579. a) Pursuit of a solo career
580. b) Jeff Lynne
581. c) "The Move Chronicles"

The Nashville Teens (Answers)

582. c) "Tobacco Road"
583. d) Durham
584. b) Arthur Sharp
585. a) "Google Eye"
586. b) John D. Loudermilk
587. d) Rhythm and Blues
588. d) "The Last Time"
589. c) "The Nashville Teens"

Nazareth (Answers)

590. c) "Exercises"
591. b) 1975
592. c) Dan McCafferty
593. d) "This Flight Tonight"
594. b) "Play 'n' the Game"
595. a) "Bad Bad Boy"
596. c) "Close Enough for Rock 'n' Roll"

The Nice (Answers Page 152)

597. Who was the keyboardist and founding member of the
1960s British rock band The Nice?
a) Keith Emerson
b) Rick Wakeman
c) Tony Kaye
d) Jon Lord

598. The Nice gained recognition for their innovative approach
to rock music, incorporating elements of classical music.
Which composer's works did they frequently reinterpret in
their arrangements?
a) Ludwig van Beethoven
b) Wolfgang Amadeus Mozart
c) Johann Sebastian Bach
d) Pyotr Ilyich Tchaikovsky

599. The Nice released a debut album in 1967 that showcased
their blending of rock and classical influences. What is the
title of this groundbreaking album?
a) "The Thoughts of Emerlist Davjack"
b) "Ars Longa Vita Brevis"
c) "Nice"
d) "Five Bridges"

600. The Nice's live performances were known for their dynamic
and theatrical nature. Which instrument did Keith Emerson
famously incorporate into his stage antics?
a) Flute
b) Theremin
c) Violin
d) Bagpipes

601. In 1969, The Nice released an album featuring a
composition that combined rock and orchestral elements.
What is the title of this album and the notable track?
a) "Five Bridges" – "Intermezzo"
b) "The Nice" – "Rondo"
c) "Ars Longa Vita Brevis" – "Symphony for the Damned"
d) "Elegy" – "Hang on to a Dream"

The Nice (Answers Page 152)

602. Which drummer was an essential member of The Nice, contributing to their powerful and dynamic sound?
a) Carl Palmer
b) Bill Bruford
c) Ginger Baker
d) Brian Davison

603. The Nice disbanded in the early 1970s, and its members pursued various musical projects. Which of the following bands did Keith Emerson join after The Nice?
a) Emerson, Lake & Palmer
b) Yes
c) King Crimson
d) Genesis

The Open Mind (Answers Page 152)

604. Who was the lead vocalist and guitarist of The Open Mind?
a) Ray Nye
b) Tim du Feu
c) Mike Brancaccio
d) Philip Fox

605. The Open Mind is best known for their 1969 single:
a) "Pictures of Matchstick Men"
b) "Magic Potion"
c) "White Rabbit"
d) "A Whiter Shade of Pale"

606. The Open Mind's music is often associated with which subgenre of rock?
a) Prog rock
b) Blues rock
c) Psychedelic rock
d) Folk rock

The Open Mind (Answers Page 152)

607. What was the title of The Open Mind's only studio album, released in 1969?
a) "Mind Games"
b) "The Open Mind"
c) "Psychedelic Dawn"
d) "Echo of the Past"

608. The Open Mind's lineup included members who later joined which other notable British rock band?
a) Cream
b) The Yardbirds
c) Deep Purple
d) Pink Floyd

The Outlaws (Answers Page 152)

609. What year was The Outlaws formed as a band?
a) 1962
b) 1964
c) 1966
d) 1968

610. Which of the following instrumental hits is associated with The Outlaws?
a) "Walk, Don't Run"
b) "Wipe Out"
c) "Apache"
d) "Sioux Serenade"

611. The Outlaws' lineup featured notable guitarist Ritchie Blackmore. What famous rock band did Blackmore later co-found?
a) The Yardbirds
b) The Rolling Stones
c) Deep Purple
d) The Kinks

The Outlaws (Answers Page 152)

612. The Outlaws often incorporated elements of which musical genre into their instrumental rock sound?
    a) Jazz
    b) Blues
    c) Country
    d) Reggae

613. The Outlaws released an album in 1964 titled:
    a) "Surfing the Shadows"
    b) "Outlawed"
    c) "Pinnacle"
    d) "Dream of the West"

614. What was the name of The Outlaws' most successful single, released in 1961?
    a) "Apache"
    b) "Sioux Serenade"
    c) "Swingin' Low"
    d) "Ambush"

615. The Outlaws' music is often associated with the instrumental rock scene known as:
    a) Merseybeat
    b) Skiffle
    c) Surf music
    d) Psychedelic rock

The Paramounts (Answers Page 152)

616. Which future Procol Harum members were part of The Paramounts?
    a) Gary Brooker and Robin Trower
    b) Keith Reid and Matthew Fisher
    c) B.J. Wilson and Chris Copping
    d) Dave Knights and Mick Brownlee

The Paramounts (Answers Page 152)

617. What was the debut single released by The Paramounts in
1964?
a) "Poison Ivy"
b) "I'm the One Who Loves You"
c) "Sharon"
d) "Just Once in My Life"

618. The Paramounts gained attention for their energetic covers
of songs by which iconic American R&B artist?
a) Chuck Berry
b) Ray Charles
c) Fats Domino
d) Bo Diddley

619. In 1966, The Paramounts released their only studio album.
What was its title?
a) "The Paramounts"
b) "Whiter Shade of Pale"
c) "Poky Little Puppy"
d) "A Whiter Shade of Paramounts"

620. Which member of The Paramounts went on to co-write the
hit song "A Whiter Shade of Pale" with Keith Reid?
a) Gary Brooker
b) Robin Trower
c) Chris Copping
d) B.J. Wilson

The Nice (Answers)

597. a) Keith Emerson
598. c) Johann Sebastian Bach
599. a) "The Thoughts of Emerlist Davjack"
600. b) Theremin
601. a) "Five Bridges" – "Intermezzo"
602. d) Brian Davison
603. a) Emerson, Lake & Palmer

The Open Mind (Answers)

604. b) Tim du Feu
605. b) "Magic Potion"
606. c) Psychedelic rock
607. b) "The Open Mind"
608. c) Deep Purple

The Outlaws (Answers)

609. b) 1964
610. d) "Sioux Serenade"
611. c) Deep Purple
612. a) Jazz
613. c) "Pinnacle"
614. c) "Swingin' Low"
615. c) Surf music

The Paramounts (Answers)

616. a) Gary Brooker and Robin Trower
617. b) "I'm the One Who Loves You
618. c) Fats Domino
619. a) "The Paramounts"
620. a) Gary Brooker

Pink Floyd (Answers Page 159)

621. What was Pink Floyd's debut studio album, released in 1967?
a) "The Dark Side of the Moon"
b) "Wish You Were Here"
c) "The Piper at the Gates of Dawn"
d) "Atom Heart Mother"

622. Which Pink Floyd album features the iconic song "Wish You Were Here"?
a) "Animals"
b) "Meddle"
c) "Dark Side of the Moon"
d) "Wish You Were Here"

623. What is the name of the lead guitarist and one of the founding members of Pink Floyd?
a) Roger Waters
b) David Gilmour
c) Nick Mason
d) Richard Wright

624. Which Pink Floyd album is known for its concept about the music industry and features the character "Pink"?
a) "The Wall"
b) "Animals"
c) "A Saucerful of Secrets"
d) "Obscured by Clouds"

625. What is the title of Pink Floyd's first chart-topping album in the United States?
a) "The Wall"
b) "Animals"
c) "The Dark Side of the Moon"
d) "Wish You Were Here"

626. Which Pink Floyd album was released in 1975 and explores the themes of alienation and social inequality?
a) "Wish You Were Here"
b) "Animals"
c) "Meddle"

d) "Atom Heart Mother"
Pink Floyd (Answers Page 159)

627. What is the title of Pink Floyd's double album released in 1970 that features a live recording on one of its discs?
a) "Obscured by Clouds"
b) "Ummagumma"
c) "Meddle"
d) "Atom Heart Mother"

628. Which Pink Floyd song features the famous line "We don't need no education"?
a) "Comfortably Numb"
b) "Another Brick in the Wall, Part 2"
c) "Money"
d) "Shine On You Crazy Diamond"

629. What is the title of Pink Floyd's final studio album, released in 2014, featuring unreleased material from the 1990s?
a) "The Division Bell"
b) "A Momentary Lapse of Reason"
c) "The Endless River"
d) "Pulse"

630. What is the title of the instrumental track that serves as the final song on Pink Floyd's album "The Wall"?
a) "Goodbye Blue Sky"
b) "Hey You"
c) "Comfortably Numb"
d) "Outside the Wall"

631. Which Pink Floyd album cover features a prism dispersing light into a spectrum of colors?
a) "Animals"
b) "Wish You Were Here"
c) "The Wall"
d) "The Dark Side of the Moon"

Pink Floyd (Answers Page 159)

632. What is the name of Pink Floyd's founding member and original principal songwriter who left the band in 1968?
a) Richard Wright
b) Syd Barrett
c) Roger Waters
d) Nick Mason

633. Pink Floyd's live album "Pulse" was recorded during which tour?
a) "Animals" Tour
b) "Wish You Were Here" Tour
c) "A Momentary Lapse of Reason" Tour
d) "The Wall" Tour

634. What is the title of Pink Floyd's 1972 soundtrack album for the film "Obscured by Clouds"?
a) "More"
b) "Ummagumma"
c) "Atom Heart Mother"
d) "Meddle"

Pinkerton's Assorted Colours (Answers Page 159)

635. What was the name of Pinkerton's Assorted Colours' first album?
a) Pinkerton's Assorted Colours did not release an album.
b) The Sorrows
c) Pink Floyd
d) The Beatles

636. Which of the following cities was Pinkerton's Assorted Colours formed in?
a) Liverpool
b) Coventry
c.) Manchester
d) London

Pinkerton's Assorted Colours (Answers Page 159)

637. Which of the following songs was a hit for Pinkerton's
Assorted Colours
a) "I Want to Hold Your Hand"
b) "Smoke Gets in Your Eyes"
c.) "Indian Reservation"
d.) "Mirror, Mirror"

638. Which of the following is NOT a member of Pinkerton's
Assorted Colours?
a) Don Fardon
b) Samuel "Pinkerton" Kempe
c) Phil Packham
d) Bruce Finlay

639. Which of the following songs was NOT recorded by
Pinkerton's Assorted Colours?
a) "Mirror, Mirror"
b) "Don't Stop Loving Me Baby"
c) "Mum and Dad"
d) "As Far as I Can See…"

Pretty Things (Answers Page 159)

640. What was the debut studio album released by the Pretty
Things in 1965?
a) "Get the Picture?"
b) "S.F. Sorrow"
c) "The Pretty Things"
d) "Parachute"

641. Which member of the Pretty Things was the lead vocalist
and a founding member of the band?
a) Dick Taylor
b) Phil May
c) Brian Pendleton
d) Skip Alan

Pretty Things (Answers Page 159)

642. The Pretty Things had a hit single in 1964 that reached the
UK Top 10. What was the title of this song?
a) "Honey, I Need"
b) "Don't Bring Me Down"
c) "Midnight to Six Man"
d) "Rosalyn"
Correct Answer:

643. In 1968, the Pretty Things released a concept album that is
often regarded as one of the first rock operas. What is the
title of this album?
a) "Parachute"
b) "S.F. Sorrow"
c) "Emotions"
d) "Silk Torpedo"

644. The Pretty Things' lead guitarist, Dick Taylor, was originally
a member of which other influential British rock band?
a) The Rolling Stones
b) The Yardbirds
c) The Who
d) The Kinks

645. What was the title of the Pretty Things' psychedelic rock
album released in 1967?
a) "Get the Picture?"
b) "S.F. Sorrow"
c) "Emotions"
d) "Parachute"

646. The Pretty Things' 1968 album "S.F. Sorrow" is often cited
as an early concept album. What is the theme of this concept
album?
a) War
b) Love
c) Aging
d) The life story of a fictional character

Pretty Things (Answers Page 159)

647. What was the title of the Pretty Things' blues-influenced studio album released in 1965?
a) "The Pretty Things"
b) "Parachute"
c) "Get the Picture?"
d) "Phil May Sings"

Pink Floyd (Answers)

621. c) "The Piper at the Gates of Dawn"
622. d) "Wish You Were Here"
623. b) David Gilmour
624. a) "The Wall"
625. c) "The Dark Side of the Moon"
626. b) "Animals"
627. b) "Ummagumma"
628. b) "Another Brick in the Wall, Part 2"
629. c) "The Endless River"
630. d) "Outside the Wall"
631. d) "The Dark Side of the Moon"
632. b) Syd Barrett
633. c) "A Momentary Lapse of Reason" Tour
634. a) "More"

Pinkerton's Assorted Colours (Answers)

635. a) Pinkerton's Assorted Colours did not release an album.
636. b) Coventry
637. d) "Mirror, Mirror"
638. a) Don Fardon
639. d) "As Far as I Can See…"

Pretty Things (Answers)

640. c) "The Pretty Things"
641. b) Phil May
642. b) "Don't Bring Me Down"
643. b) "S.F. Sorrow"
644. a) The Rolling Stones
645. c) "Emotions"
646. d) The life story of a fictional character
647. c) "Get the Picture?"

Procol Harum (Answers Page 167)

648. What was Procol Harum's breakthrough single released in
1967 that became a global hit?
a) "Conquistador"
b) "Shine On Brightly"
c) "A Whiter Shade of Pale"
d) "Homburg"

649. Who was the lead singer and primary lyricist for Procol
Harum during the 1960s and 1970s?
a) Gary Brooker
b) Robin Trower
c) Matthew Fisher
d) Keith Reid
Correct Answer:

650. What was the title of Procol Harum's debut studio album,
released in 1967?
a) "Shine On Brightly"
b) "A Salty Dog"
c) "Procol Harum"
d) "Home"

651. Procol Harum's second album, released in 1968, featured the
hit single "Homburg." What was the title of this album?
a) "A Salty Dog"
b) "Shine On Brightly"
c) "Home"
d) "Procol Harum"

652. Which instrument did Matthew Fisher play in Procol Harum
and was known for his distinctive sound on "A Whiter Shade
of Pale"?
a) Organ
b) Guitar
c) Piano
d) Flute

Procol Harum (Answers Page 167)

653. Procol Harum's 1972 album "Procol's Ninth" marked the return of a former member. Who rejoined the band for this album?
a) Matthew Fisher
b) Robin Trower
c) David Knights
d) Keith Reid

Quatermass (Answers Page 167)

654. Who was the keyboardist and vocalist for Quatermass?
a) Mick Farren
b) J. Peter Robinson
c) John Gustafson
d) Pete Sears

655. Quatermass is known for blending progressive rock with elements of which other musical genre?
a) Jazz
b) Country
c) Punk
d) Blues

656. The self-titled debut album by Quatermass was released in which year?
a) 1968
b) 1969
c) 1970
d) 1971

657. What is the title of Quatermass's most well-known song, which has been covered by various artists?
a) "Black Sheep of the Family"
b) "One Blind Mice"
c) "Quatermass"
d) "Gemini"

Quatermass (Answers Page 167)

658. After the disbandment of Quatermass, John Gustafson
joined which well-known British rock band?
a) Yes
b) Deep Purple
c) The Rolling Stones
d) Genesis

The Rockin' Berries (Answers Page 167)

659. The Rockin' Berries had a hit single in 1964 that reached the
UK Top 10. What was the title of this song?
a) "He's in Town"
b) "Poor Man's Son"
c) "Smile"
d) "What in the World's Come Over You"

660. In addition to their musical career, the Rockin' Berries were
also known for their comedic performances on which British
TV show in the 1960s?
a) "Top of the Pops"
b) "The Ed Sullivan Show"
c) "The Benny Hill Show"
d) "Ready Steady Go!"

661. The Rockin' Berries covered a classic song originally
recorded by Chuck Berry. What was the title of this song?
a) "Sweet Little Sixteen"
b) "Roll Over Beethoven"
c) "Johnny B. Goode"
d) "Maybellene"

662. What was the name of the Rockin' Berries' debut album,
released in 1964?
a) "Life Is Just a Bowl of Berries"
b) "In Town"
c) "What in the World's Come Over You"
d) "Poor Man's Son"

The Rockin' Berries (Answers Page 167)

663. The Rockin' Berries achieved success with their cover of a
     song by Bobby Vee. What was the title of this song?
     a) "The Basket of Berries"
     b) "Hitch Hike"
     c) "Poor Man's Son"
     d) "He's in Town"

664. Which member of the Rockin' Berries went on to have a
     successful solo career, earning hits like "Jennifer Eccles" and
     "Lily the Pink"?
     a) Geoff Turton
     b) Chuck Botfield
     c) Clive Lea
     d) Terry Bond

665. The Rockin' Berries' song "What in the World's Come Over
     You" was a cover of a hit by which American artist?
     a) Roy Orbison
     b) Jack Scott
     c) Ricky Nelson
     d) Paul Anka

The Rolling Stones (Answers Page 167)

666. What was the Rolling Stones' debut studio album, released in
     1964?
     a) "Out of Our Heads"
     b) "Aftermath"
     c) "Beggars Banquet"
     d) "The Rolling Stones"

667. Which member of the Rolling Stones played the harmonica
     and was known for his energetic stage presence?
     a) Mick Jagger
     b) Keith Richards
     c) Brian Jones
     d) Charlie Watts

The Rolling Stones (Answers Page 167)

668. The Rolling Stones' first UK No. 1 hit single, released in 1964, was a cover of which song?
a) "Paint It, Black"
b) "Time Is on My Side"
c) "I Wanna Be Your Man"
d) "Satisfaction"

669. What was the title of the Rolling Stones' iconic 1968 album that featured the song "Sympathy for the Devil"?
a) "Beggars Banquet"
b) "Sticky Fingers"
c) "Let It Bleed"
d) "Their Satanic Majesties Request"

670. The Rolling Stones' classic album "Sticky Fingers" (1971) featured the famous tongue and lips logo. Who designed this iconic logo?
a) Andy Warhol
b) Peter Blake
c) David Bailey
d) John Pasche

671. In 1969, the Rolling Stones organized a free concert in Hyde Park as a tribute to their former bandmate Brian Jones. What was the name of this historic event?
a) "Rock and Roll Circus"
b) "Altamont Free Concert"
c) "Summer of Love"
d) "Stones in the Park"

672. What was the title of the Rolling Stones' album released in 1965 that included the hit single "(I Can't Get No) Satisfaction"?
a) "Out of Our Heads"
b) "Let It Bleed"
c) "Between the Buttons"
d) "Aftermath"

The Rolling Stones (Answers Page 167)

673. The Rolling Stones' song "Paint It, Black" (1966) featured a prominent instrument that was unusual for rock music. What instrument was it?
a) Sitar
b) Bagpipes
c) Flute
d) Harpsichord

674. What was the title of the Rolling Stones' album released in 1972 that included the hit single "Angie"?
a) "Exile on Main St."
b) "Goats Head Soup"
c) "Some Girls"
d) "Sticky Fingers"

675. The Rolling Stones' 1969 album "Let It Bleed" featured a cover of a classic song by which blues artist?
a) Muddy Waters
b) Howlin' Wolf
c) Robert Johnson
d) Son House

676. What was the title of the Rolling Stones' 1966 album that included the hit single "19th Nervous Breakdown"?
a) "Between the Buttons"
b) "Out of Our Heads"
c) "Aftermath"
d) "Between the Buttons"

677. The Rolling Stones' 1978 album "Some Girls" featured a controversial cover with cutout faces of celebrities. Who designed this cover?
a) Peter Blake
b) Andy Warhol
c) David Bailey
d) Hubert Kretzschmar

The Rolling Stones (Answers Page 167)

678. The Rolling Stones' "Steel Wheels" (1989) marked the return of which former band member?
a) Brian Jones
b) Mick Taylor
c) Bill Wyman
d) Ian Stewart

Procol Harum (Answers)

648. c) "A Whiter Shade of Pale"
649. a) Gary Brooker
650. c) "Procol Harum"
651. b) "Shine On Brightly"
652. a) Organ
653. b) Robin Trower

Quatermass (Answers)

654. b) J. Peter Robinson
655. a) Jazz
656. c) 1970
657. a) "Black Sheep of the Family"
658. b) Deep Purple

The Rockin' Berries (Answers)

659. a) "He's in Town"
660. c) "The Benny Hill Show"
661. b) "Roll Over Beethoven"
662. a) "Life Is Just a Bowl of Berries"
663. c) "Poor Man's Son"
664. a) Geoff Turton
665. b) Jack Scott

The Rolling Stones (Answers)

666. d) "The Rolling Stones"
667. a) Mick Jagger
668. c) "I Wanna Be Your Man"
669. d) "Their Satanic Majesties Request"
670. d) John Pasche
671. d) "Stones in the Park"
672. a) "Out of Our Heads"
673. a) Sitar
674. b) "Goats Head Soup"
675. a) Muddy Waters
676. a) "Between the Buttons"
677. d) Hubert Kretzschmar

678. b) Mick Taylor
The Searchers (Answers Page 174)

679. The Searchers, a 1960s British rock band, had a hit single with a cover of a classic song by The Drifters. What is the title of this song?
a) "Needles and Pins"
b) "Love Potion No. 9"
c) "Sweets for My Sweet"
d) "Sugar and Spice"

680. The Searchers gained popularity during the Merseybeat era. Which city served as the band's hometown during their early years?
a) Liverpool
b) Manchester
c) Birmingham
d) London
Correct Answer:

681. What was the title of The Searchers' debut album, released in 1963?
a) "Meet The Searchers"
b) "Take Me for What I'm Worth"
c) "Sounds Like Searchers"
d) "Sugar and Spice"

682. The Searchers had a major hit in 1964 with the song "Needles and Pins." Who co-wrote this song along with Jack Nitzsche?
a) Gerry Goffin and Carole King
b) Burt Bacharach and Hal David
c) John Lennon and Paul McCartney
d) Sonny Bono and Jack Nitzsche

683. What was distinctive about The Searchers' version of "Love Potion No. 9," released in 1965?
a) It featured a sitar solo.
b) It was sung entirely in French.
c) It had a prominent use of a 12-string guitar.
d) It included a spoken-word section.

The Searchers (Answers Page 174)

684. The Searchers' lineup underwent changes over the years.
Who was the lead vocalist and rhythm guitarist of the band
during their most successful period?
a) Mike Pender
b) Tony Jackson
c) Frank Allen
d) John McNally

685. The Searchers were known for their covers of American
rock and roll songs. Which Elvis Presley hit did they cover
and release as a single in 1963?
a) "Heartbreak Hotel"
b) "All Shook Up"
c) "Hound Dog"
d) "Don't Be Cruel"

The Shadows (Answers Page 174)

686. The Shadows, a British instrumental rock band of the 1960s,
originally started as the backing band for which legendary
British singer?
a) Cliff Richard
b) Billy Fury
c) Adam Faith
d) Marty Wilde

687. What was The Shadows' first major hit single, released in
1960?
a) "Apache"
b) "Wonderful Land"
c) "Kon-Tiki"
d) "Foot Tapper"

688. The Shadows' guitarist Hank Marvin was known for his
distinctive sound and playing style. Which guitar did he
famously use during the band's early years?
a) Fender Stratocaster
b) Gibson Les Paul
c) Gretsch Country Gentleman

d) Rickenbacker 360

The Shadows (Answers Page 174)

689. The Shadows had a hit single in 1961 that featured a catchy dance beat and became a signature tune. What is the title of this instrumental track?
a) "Dance On!"
b) "Atlantis"
c) "FBI"
d) "The Savage"

690. What was the title of The Shadows' debut album, released in 1961?
a) "The Shadows"
b) "Out of the Shadows"
c) "Shadow Music"
d) "Dance with The Shadows"

691. In 1963, The Shadows released a single that showcased their versatility with vocals. Who sang lead on the hit song "Foot Tapper"?
a) Bruce Welch
b) Hank Marvin
c) Brian Bennett
d) John Rostill

692. The Shadows were known for their collaborations with Cliff Richard. What was the title of the musical film in which they starred alongside Cliff Richard in 1961?
a) "Summer Holiday"
b) "The Young Ones"
c) "Expresso Bongo"
d) "Wonderful to Be Young"

693. Which member of The Shadows composed several of their hit songs, including "Apache" and "Man of Mystery"?
a) Brian Bennett
b) Bruce Welch
c) Jet Harris
d) Hank Marvin

The Shadows (Answers Page 174)

694. The Shadows' 1960s repertoire included a cover of the theme from a popular Western film. What is the title of this instrumental track?
a) "The Alamo"
b) "The Good, the Bad and the Ugly"
c) "Gunfight at the O.K. Corral"
d) "Shane"

695. The Shadows released an album in 1963 that included the hit single "Atlantis." What is the title of this album?
a) "Shadows Are Go!"
b) "Shadows in the Night"
c) "Out of the Shadows"
d) "Dance with The Shadows"

696. The Shadows had a resurgence in popularity in the 1970s and 1980s. What song, released in 1977, became a hit for the band and featured a vocal performance by Hank Marvin?
a) "Theme from The Deer Hunter"
b) "Don't Cry for Me Argentina"
c) "Riders in the Sky"
d) "Don't Cry for Me, Argentina"

Skin Alley (Answers Page 174)

697. Who were the founding members of Skin Alley?
a) Thomas Crimble and Alvin Pope
b) Krzysztof Henryk Justkiewicz and Tony Knight
c) Nick Graham and Bob James
d) Tom Martin and Dave Watts

698. Skin Alley's music is often characterized by a fusion of:
a) Psychedelic rock and blues
b) Jazz and funk
c) Folk and country
d) Progressive rock and punk

Skin Alley (Answers Page 174)

699. What was the title of Skin Alley's debut album, released in 1969?
    a) "Two Quid Deal"
    b) "To Pagham & Beyond"
    c) "Skin Deep"
    d) "Big Brother Is Watching You"

700. Skin Alley briefly disbanded in the early 1970s but reunited later. During their reunion, they released an album with a title referencing a famous novel by George Orwell. What was the title?
    a) "Animal Farm"
    b) "1984"
    c) "Brave New World"
    d) "A Clockwork Orange"

701. Which of the following labels released Skin Alley's albums during their career?
    a) Apple Records
    b) Vertigo Records
    c) Island Records
    d) Deram Records

The Small Faces (Answers Page 174)

702. The Small Faces were formed in 1965 and hailed from which city in England?
    a) Liverpool
    b) London
    c) Manchester
    d) Birmingham

703. What was the title of the Small Faces' debut studio album, released in 1966?
    a) "Ogdens' Nut Gone Flake"
    b) "Small Faces"
    c) "There Are But Four Small Faces"
    d) "From the Beginning"

The Small Faces (Answers Page 174)

704. Who was the lead singer and songwriter for the Small Faces?
    a) Steve Marriott
    b) Ronnie Lane
    c) Kenney Jones
    d) Ian McLagan

705. The Small Faces had a hit single in 1967 and reached #3 on
    the UK Singles Chart. What was the title of the song?
    a) "Itchycoo Park"
    b) "Lazy Sunday"
    c) "Tin Soldier"
    d) "All or Nothing"

706. In 1968, the Small Faces released an album that's considered
    a psychedelic classic. What's the title of the album?
    a) "Small Faces"
    b) "Ogdens' Nut Gone Flake"
    c) "There Are But Four Small Faces"
    d) "From the Beginning"

707. The Small Faces underwent a lineup change in 1969 when
    two members left to form Humble Pie. Who were these
    departing members?
    a) Steve Marriott and Ronnie Lane
    b) Ian McLagan and Kenney Jones
    c) Steve Marriott and Kenney Jones
    d) Ronnie Lane and Ian McLagan

708. What instrument did Ronnie Lane play in the Small Faces?
    a) Guitar
    b) Bass
    c) Drums
    d) Keyboards

709. The Small Faces reunited in the 1970s with a new lead
    singer. Who replaced Steve Marriott?
    a) Rod Stewart
    b) Chris Farlowe
    c) Paul Rodgers

d) Robert Plant

The Searchers (Answers)

679. c) "Sweets for My Sweet"
680. a) Liverpool
681. a) "Meet The Searchers"
682. d) Sonny Bono and Jack Nitzsche
683. a) It featured a sitar solo.
684. a) Mike Pender
685. c) "Hound Dog"

The Shadows (Answers)

686. a) Cliff Richard
687. a) "Apache"
688. a) Fender Stratocaster
689. a) "Dance On!"
690. b) "Out of the Shadows"
691. a) Bruce Welch
692. a) "Summer Holiday"
693. d) Hank Marvin
694. c) "Gunfight at the O.K. Corral"
695. a) "Shadows Are Go!"
696. c) "Riders in the Sky"

Skin Alley (Answers)

697. a) Thomas Crimble and Alvin Pope
698. b) Jazz and funk
699. c) "Skin Deep"
700. b) "1984"
701. d) Deram Records

The Small Faces (Answers)

702. b) London
703. b) "Small Faces"
704. a) Steve Marriott
705. d) "All or Nothing"
706. b) "Ogdens' Nut Gone Flake"
707. b) Ian McLagan and Kenney Jones
708. b) Bass

709. a) Rod Stewart

The Smoke (Answers Page 180)

710. What was the name of The Smoke's biggest hit?
 a) "My Friend Jack"
 b) "High In A Room"
 c) "If The Weather's Sunny"
 d) "We Can Take It"

711. What was the original name of The Smoke?
 a) The Moonshots
 b) The Shots
 c) Tony Adams and the Viceroys
 d). The Smoke

712. Which member of The Smoke was the lead vocalist?
 a) Mal Luker
 b) John "Zeke" Lund
 c) Geoff Gill
 d) Mick Rowley

713. What was the name of The Smoke's first single?
 a) "Keep A Hold Of What You've Got"
 b) "She's A Liar"
 c) "There She Goes"
 d) "Walk Right Out The Door"

714. What was the name of The Smoke's debut album?
 a) "It's Smoke Time"
 b) "My Friend Jack"
 c) "High In A Room"
 d) "If The Weather's Sunny"

715. What was the name of the band that included John "Zeke"
 Lund, Mal Luker, and Geoff Gill before they formed The
 Smoke?
 a) The Moonshots
 b) The Shots
 c) Tony Adams and the Viceroys
 d) The Smoke

The Smoke (Answers Page 180)

716. What was the reason behind the BBC banning airplay of
The Smoke's hit song "My Friend Jack"?
a) It was too long
b) It was too loud
c) It was too controversial
d) It had drug references

Soft Machine (Answers Page 180)

717. Soft Machine was a pioneering British psychedelic and
progressive rock band formed in the mid-1960s. Which city
is often associated with the birth of the band?
a) London
b) Liverpool
c) Manchester
d) Canterbury

718. What was the original name of Soft Machine when they
formed in 1966?
a) Wilde Flowers
b) Pink Floyd
c) Caravan
d) Gong

719. Soft Machine was known for its fusion of rock, jazz, and
avant-garde music. Which member of the band played
saxophone and became a key figure in its jazz-oriented
sound?
a) Robert Wyatt
b) Kevin Ayers
c) Mike Ratledge
d) Elton Dean

720. Soft Machine's debut album, released in 1968, was titled:
a) "Third"
b) "Soft Machine"
c) "Volume Two"
d) "The Soft Machine"

Soft Machine (Answers Page 180)

721. What drummer and vocalist was an original member of Soft
Machine and later became known for his work with
Matching Mole?
a) Phil Collins
b) Robert Wyatt
c) Carl Palmer
d) Bill Bruford

722. Soft Machine's third studio album, released in 1970, is often
considered a landmark in progressive rock. What is the title
of this album?
a) "Third"
b) "Fourth"
c) "Fifth"
d) "Six"

723. Which influential guitarist joined Soft Machine in 1972,
bringing a fusion of jazz and rock elements to the band?
a) Allan Holdsworth
b) Robert Fripp
c) John McLaughlin
d) Steve Howe

724. Soft Machine's original bassist, who also played keyboard
and sang, left the band in the late 1960s. Who was this
founding member?
a) Hugh Hopper
b) Mike Ratledge
c) Kevin Ayers
d) Daevid Allen

The Sorrows (Answers Page 180)

725. Which of the following cities was The Sorrows formed in?
a) Liverpool
b) Coventry
c) Manchester
d) London

The Sorrows (Answers Page 180)

726. What was the name of The Sorrows' first album?
    a) Take a Heart
    b) The Sorrows
    c) Pink Floyd
    d) The Beatles

727. Which of the following is NOT a member of The Sorrows?
    a) Don Fardon
    b) Rod Argent
    c) Phil Packham
    d) Bruce Finlay

728. Which of the following songs was a hit for The Sorrows?
    a) "I Want to Hold Your Hand"
    b) "Smoke Gets in Your Eyes"
    c) "Indian Reservation"
    d) "Take a Heart"

729. Which album was NOT recorded by The Sorrows?
    a) Take a Heart
    b) Teenage Head
    c) Old Songs, New Songs
    d) As Far as I Can See…

Spooky Tooth (Answers Page 180)

730. Spooky Tooth, a British rock band formed in the 1960s, was known for their bluesy and progressive sound. Who was the original lead singer of Spooky Tooth?
    a) Mike Harrison
    b) Gary Wright
    c) Luther Grosvenor
    d) Greg Ridley

731. In 1968, Spooky Tooth released their debut album, featuring a cover of a song by which legendary blues artist?
    a) Howlin' Wolf
    b) Muddy Waters
    c) John Lee Hooker

d) Son House

Spooky Tooth (Answers Page 180)

732. Which Spooky Tooth album, released in 1969, is often
considered one of their finest works and includes tracks like
"Better by You, Better Than Me"?
a) "Spooky Two"
b) "Ceremony"
c) "It's All About"
d) "The Last Puff"

733. Spooky Tooth's keyboardist, known for his distinctive voice
and later solo hits like "Dream Weaver," joined the band in
1969. What is his name?
a) Gary Wright
b) Luther Grosvenor
c) Greg Ridley
d) Mike Kellie

734. Spooky Tooth collaborated with which famous musician and
producer on the album "Spooky Two"?
a) George Martin
b) Jimmy Miller
c) Phil Spector
d) Glyn Johns

735. Spooky Tooth's 1973 album "You Broke My Heart So I
Busted Your Jaw" featured a cover of a song by which iconic
singer-songwriter?
a) Bob Dylan
b) Leonard Cohen
c) Joni Mitchell
d) Neil Young

736. After disbanding in the early 1970s, Spooky Tooth reunited
in the 1990s. Which of their original members was part of
this reunion?
a) Mike Harrison
b) Gary Wright
c) Luther Grosvenor
d) Mike Kellie

The Smoke (Answers)

710. a) "My Friend Jack"
711. b) The Shots
712. d) Mick Rowley
713. a) "Keep A Hold Of What You've Got"
714. a) "It's Smoke Time"
715. a) The Moonshots
716. d) It had drug references

Soft Machine (Answers)

717. d) Canterbury
718. a) Wilde Flowers
719. d) Elton Dean
720. c) "Volume Two"
721. b) Robert Wyatt
722. a) "Third"
723. a) Allan Holdsworth
724. c) Kevin Ayers

The Sorrows (Answers)

725. b) Coventry
726. a) Take a Heart
727. b) Rod Argent
728. d) "Take a Heart"
729. d) As Far as I Can See…

Spooky Tooth (Answers)

730. a) Mike Harrison
731. b) Muddy Waters
732. a) "Spooky Two"
733. a) Gary Wright
734. b) Jimmy Miller
735. d) Neil Young
736. a) Mike Harrison

Status Quo (Answers Page 187)

737. Who are the original founding members of Status Quo?
    a) Francis Rossi and Rick Parfitt
    b) Alan Lancaster and John Coghlan
    c) Francis Rossi and Alan Lancaster
    d) Rick Parfitt and John Coghlan

738. Status Quo's breakthrough hit single, released in 1968, is titled:
    a) "Pictures of Matchstick Men"
    b) "Down Down"
    c) "Rockin' All Over the World"
    d) "Caroline"

739. In the 1970s, Status Quo became known for their distinctive music style, often referred to as:
    a) Boogie rock
    b) Prog rock
    c) Glam rock
    d) Folk rock

740. Which album marked a significant change in Status Quo's sound, introducing the boogie rock style?
    a) "Hello!"
    b) "Blue for You"
    c) "Piledriver"
    d) "Ma Kelly's Greasy Spoon"

741. Status Quo's iconic "double-neck" guitar was often played by:
    a) Francis Rossi
    b) Rick Parfitt
    c) Alan Lancaster
    d) John Coghlan

742. In 1985, Status Quo opened the Live Aid concert at Wembley Stadium with a performance of which song?
    a) "In the Army Now"
    b) "Roll Over Lay Down"
    c) "Whatever You Want"

d) "Rockin' All Over the World"

Status Quo (Answers Page 187)

743. Status Quo's classic line-up featured the "Frantic Four."
Who were the members of the Frantic Four?
a) Rossi, Parfitt, Lancaster, Coghlan
b) Rossi, Parfitt, Edwards, Kirke
c) Rossi, Parfitt, Bown, Bolder
d) Rossi, Parfitt, Rhino, Matt Letley

Steeleye Span (Answers Page 187)

744. Who was the founding member and lead vocalist of Steeleye
Span, the British folk-rock band formed in the late 1960s?
a) Maddy Prior
b) Tim Hart
c) Peter Knight
d) Rick Kemp

745. Steeleye Span achieved commercial success with their 1975
hit single "All Around My Hat." What traditional folk tune
did they adapt for this song?
a) "Gaudete"
b) "The Blacksmith"
c) "The Lark in the Morning"
d) "Long Lankin"

746. Along With Maddy Prior, which founding member of
Steeleye Span played a significant role in the band's folk-rock
sound with his skills on the mandolin and other instruments?
a) Martin Carthy
b) Peter Knight
c) Tim Hart
d) Rick Kemp

747. Steeleye Span's album "Hark! The Village Wait" (1970) is
notable for being one of the first folk-rock albums of its
kind. Who produced this landmark album?
a) Martin Carthy
b) Ashley Hutchings
c) Joe Boyd
d) Sandy Denny

Steeleye Span (Answers Page 187)

748. Which traditional folk song, covered by Steeleye Span, tells the tale of a murderous jester and is often associated with their early repertoire?
a) "Thomas the Rhymer"
b) "The Dark-Eyed Sailor"
c) "John Barleycorn"
d) "Jigs and Reels"

Rod Stewart (Answers Page 187)

749. What was the title of Rod Stewart's debut solo album, released in 1969?
a) "Every Picture Tells a Story"
b) "Gasoline Alley"
c) "An Old Raincoat Won't Ever Let You Down"
d) "Never a Dull Moment"

750. Before his solo career, Rod Stewart was a member of which British rock group in the 1960s?
a) The Hollies
b) The Kinks
c) The Small Faces
d) The Animals

751. Rod Stewart released a hit single in 1971 that became one of his signature songs. What was the title of this song?
a) "Maggie May"
b) "You Wear It Well"
c) "Sailing"
d) "Tonight's the Night (Gonna Be Alright)"

752. In 1975, Rod Stewart released an album that marked a departure from his rock sound, embracing a disco-influenced style. What was the title of this album?
a) "Atlantic Crossing"
b) "A Night on the Town"
c) "Blondes Have More Fun"
d) "Foot Loose & Fancy Free"

Rod Stewart (Answers Page 187)

753. What was the title of Rod Stewart's first solo single, released in 1969?
a) "Handbags and Gladrags"
b) "You're in My Heart (The Final Acclaim)"
c) "Reason to Believe"
d) "Street Fighting Man"

754. Rod Stewart's album "Every Picture Tells a Story" (1971) featured a cover of a classic song by which artist?
a) Bob Dylan
b) Van Morrison
c) Cat Stevens
d) Chuck Berry

755. What is the title of the Rod Stewart album released in 1973 that included the hit single "You Wear It Well"?
a) "Never a Dull Moment"
b) "Smiler"
c) "Sing It Again Rod"
d) "A Night on the Town"

756. Rod Stewart was known for his distinctive raspy voice. Which nickname is often associated with him due to his vocal style?
a) The Crooner
b) The Voice
c) The Soul Man
d) The Modfather

757. In 1972, Rod Stewart released a double album that included the popular track "Maggie May." What was the title of this album?
a) "Every Picture Tells a Story"
b) "Gasoline Alley"
c) "Never a Dull Moment"
d) "Rod Stewart and Faces"

Rod Stewart (Answers Page 187)

758. Rod Stewart's collaboration with The Faces produced the hit single "Stay with Me." Who was the lead guitarist of The Faces?
a) Ron Wood
b) Jeff Beck
c) Mick Taylor
d) Jimmy Page

Stone The Crows (Answers Page 187)

759. Who was the lead vocalist of Stone the Crows?
a) Maggie Bell
b) Les Harvey
c) Jimmy McCulloch
d) Colin Allen

760. Stone the Crows was known for its powerful and soulful lead vocals. In addition to Maggie Bell, which member provided backing vocals and played organ?
a) Les Harvey
b) Jimmy McCulloch
c) Ronnie Leahy
d) Colin Allen

761. Tragically, Les Harvey, the guitarist of Stone the Crows, died during a performance in 1972. How did he pass away?
a) Drug overdose
b) Electrocution on stage
c) Plane crash
d) Car accident

762. Stone the Crows' music is often characterized by the fusion of blues rock with elements of:
a) Jazz
b) Reggae
c) Punk
d) Country

Stone The Crows (Answers Page 187)

763. What was the title of Stone the Crows' debut album, released in 1970?
a) "Ontinuous Performance"
b) "Teenage Licks"
c) "Ode to John Law"
d) "Stone the Crows"

764. Stone the Crows released a live album recorded at the Montreux Jazz Festival. What was the title of this album?
a) "Stone the Crows in Montreux"
b) "Live Crows"
c) "The Crows Take Flight"
d) "Ontinuous Performance Live"

765. After Stone the Crows disbanded, Maggie Bell pursued a solo career and collaborated with which ex-Free guitarist?
a) Paul Kossoff
b) Paul Rodgers
c) Andy Fraser
d) Simon Kirke

Status Quo (Answers)

737. c) Francis Rossi and Alan Lancaster
738. a) "Pictures of Matchstick Men"
739. a) Boogie rock
740. c) "Piledriver"
741. a) Francis Rossi
742. d) "Rockin' All Over the World"
743. a) Rossi, Parfitt, Lancaster, Coghlan

Steeleye Span (Answers)

744. a) Maddy Prior
745. d) "Long Lankin"
746. b) Peter Knight
747. c) Joe Boyd
748. a) "Thomas the Rhymer"

Rod Stewart (Answers)

749. c) "An Old Raincoat Won't Ever Let You Down"
750. c) The Small Faces
751. a) "Maggie May"
752. c) "Blondes Have More Fun"
753. c) "Reason to Believe"
754. a) Bob Dylan
755. b) "Smiler"
756. b) The Voice
757. a) "Every Picture Tells a Story"
758. a) Ron Wood

Stone The Crows (Answers)

759. a) Maggie Bell
760. c) Ronnie Leahy
761. b) Electrocution on stage
762. a) Jazz
763. a) "Ontinuous Performance"
764. c) "The Crows Take Flight"
765. a) Paul Kossoff

Rory Storm and The Hurricanes (Answers Page 193)

766. Rory Storm and the Hurricanes were a Liverpool-based band in the 1960s. Which future Beatles drummer was a member of this band before joining The Beatles?
a) Ringo Starr
b) Pete Best
c) Stuart Sutcliffe
d) Jimmy Nicol

767. What was the real name of Rory Storm, the lead singer and namesake of the band?
a) Rory Harrison
b) Rory O'Connor
c) Rory McManus
d) Rory Caldwell

768. Rory Storm and the Hurricanes were a popular act on the Liverpool music scene. Which famous venue did they frequently perform at alongside other Merseybeat bands?
a) The Cavern Club
b) The Marquee Club
c) The Whisky a Go Go
d) The Roxy

769. Rory Storm's energetic stage presence was often compared to which American rock and roll legend?
a) Elvis Presley
b) Chuck Berry
c) Little Richard
d) Buddy Holly

770. Which Beatles song was originally recorded by Rory Storm and the Hurricanes before The Beatles included it on their debut album "Please Please Me"?
a) "Twist and Shout"
b) "I Saw Her Standing There"
c) "Love Me Do"
d) "Roll Over Beethoven"

Rory Storm and The Hurricanes (Answers Page 193)

771. In 1960, Rory Storm and the Hurricanes toured Hamburg,
Germany, where they shared the stage with The Beatles.
What was the name of the club where they performed?
a) The Top Ten Club
b) The Star Club
c) The Kaiserkeller
d) The Indra

772. Tragically, Rory Storm passed away in 1972 at a young age.
What was the cause of his death?
a) Car accident
b) Drug overdose
c) Heart attack
d) Drowning

The Strawbs (Answers Page 193)

773. In which country were The Strawbs formed in 1964?
a) England
b) Ireland
c) Australia
d) United States

774. Which type of music are The Strawbs best known for?
a) Punk
b) Hip Hop
c.) Folk rock
d) Heavy metal

775. Which female vocalist was briefly a member of The Strawbs
in 1968?
a) Maddy Prior
b) Stevie Nicks
c) Grace Slick
d) Janis Joplin

The Strawbs (Answers Page 193)

776. Which famous keyboardist was a member of The Strawbs in
the early 1970s?
a) Rick Wakeman
b) Keith Emerson
c) Jon Lord
d) Tony Banks

777. What was the name of The Strawbs' first album?
a) Take a Heart
b) Strawbs
c) Pink Floyd
d) The Beatles

778. Which of the following songs was a hit for The Strawbs?
a) "I Want to Hold Your Hand"
b) "Smoke Gets in Your Eyes"
c) "Indian Reservation"
d) "Lay Down" Answer:

779. Which album by The Strawbs was released in 1974 and
features the hit single "Part of the Union"?
a) Bursting at the Seams
b) Hero and Heroine
c) Ghosts
d). Nomadness Answer:

The Swinging Blue Jeans (Answers Page 193)

780. The Swinging Blue Jeans were part of the Merseybeat
movement in the 1960s. What city is often associated with
the Merseybeat sound?
a) London
b) Manchester
c) Liverpool
d) Birmingham

The Swinging Blue Jeans (Answers Page 193)

781. What was the Swinging Blue Jeans' breakthrough hit single, released in 1963, that reached the Top 10 in the UK and the US?
a) "Good Golly Miss Molly"
b) "Hippy Hippy Shake"
c) "You're No Good"
d) "Don't Make Me Over"

782. The Swinging Blue Jeans covered a song originally recorded by Little Richard for their hit single. What was the title of this song?
a) "Good Golly Miss Molly"
b) "Long Tall Sally"
c) "Tutti Frutti"
d) "Lucille"

783. The Swinging Blue Jeans' original lead singer left the band in the mid-1960s. Who replaced him as the lead vocalist?
a) Ray Ennis
b) Ralph Ellis
c) Les Braid
d) Alan Lovell

784. In addition to their musical career, the Swinging Blue Jeans appeared in a British musical comedy film released in 1964. What was the title of this film?
a) "A Hard Day's Night"
b) "Help!"
c) "What's New Pussycat?"
d) "Just for Fun"

785. The Swinging Blue Jeans' 1964 album featured a cover of a hit song by Del Shannon. What was the title of this album?
a) "Hippy Hippy Shake"
b) "Blue Jeans a'Swinging"
c) "Shake with The Swinging Blue Jeans"
d) "You're No Good"

The Swinging Blue Jeans (Answers Page 193)

786. The Swinging Blue Jeans were part of the British Invasion in the United States. Which American TV show did they perform on during their U.S. tour in the 1960s?
a) "The Ed Sullivan Show"
b) "American Bandstand"
c) "The Tonight Show Starring Johnny Carson"
d) "Soul Train"

787. What was the Swinging Blue Jeans' last Top 40 hit in the UK, released in 1966?
a) "Hippy Hippy Shake"
b) "Good Golly Miss Molly"
c) "Don't Make Me Over"
d) "You're No Good"

Them (Answers Page 193)

788. What was the name of Them's lead singer?
a) Van Morrison
b) Eric Burdon
c) Mick Jagger
d) Jim Morrison

789. What was the name of Them's first single?
a) Gloria
b) Here Comes the Night
c) Mystic Eyes
d) Baby Please Don't Go

790. What was the name of Them's second album?
a) Them Again
b) The Angry Young Them
c) Them in Reality
d) Them's Secret

791. What was the name of Them's guitarist?
a) Van Morrison
b) Billy Harrison
c) Alan Henderson

d) Ray Elliott

Rory Storm and The Hurricanes (Answers)

766. b) Pete Best
767. c) Rory McManus
768. a) The Cavern Club
769. c) Little Richard
770. b) "I Saw Her Standing There"
771. b) The Star Club
772. d) Drowning

The Strawbs (Answers)

773. a) England
774. c) Folk rock
775. a) Maddy Prior
776. a) Rick Wakeman
777. b) Strawbs
778. d) "Lay Down"
779. a) Bursting at the Seams

The Swinging Blue Jeans (Answers)

780. c) Liverpool
781. b) "Hippy Hippy Shake"
782. a) "Good Golly Miss Molly"
783. d) Alan Lovell
784. d) "Just for Fun"
785. c) "Shake with The Swinging Blue Jeans"
786. a) "The Ed Sullivan Show"
787. c) "Don't Make Me Over"

Them (Answers)

788. a) Van Morrison
789. d) Baby Please Don't Go
790. b) The Angry Young Them
791. b) Billy Harrison

Toe Fat (Answers Page 198)

792. Which former Uriah Heep members were part of Toe Fat?
  a) David Byron and Ken Hensley
  b) Mick Box and Lee Kerslake
  c) Paul Newton and Keith Baker
  d) Gary Thain and John Konas

793. What was the title of Toe Fat's self-titled debut album, released in 1970?
  a) "Toe Jam"
  b) "Toe the Line"
  c) "Toe the Fat"
  d) "Toe Fat"

794. Toe Fat's music is often associated with which rock genre?
  a) Progressive rock
  b) Psychedelic rock
  c) Blues rock
  d) Folk rock

795. In addition to their self-titled debut, Toe Fat released a second album in 1971. What was the title of this album?
  a) "Bad Side of the Moon"
  b) "Toe Fat Two"
  c) "Toe Fat Strikes Again"
  d) "Two Feet"

Tomorrow (Answers Page 198)

796. Tomorrow is best known for their 1967 single:
  a) "White Rabbit"
  b) "Sunshine of Your Love"
  c) "My White Bicycle"
  d) "Purple Haze"

797. Which Tomorrow member later became a founding member of the supergroup Yes?
  a) Steve Howe
  b) Keith West
  c) John "Twink" Alder

d) Junior Wood

Tomorrow (Answers Page 198)

798. Tomorrow's self-titled debut album was released in:
   a) 1965
   b) 1967
   c) 1969
   d) 1971

799. Tomorrow was part of the Swinging London scene and was associated with which cultural movement?
   a) Beat Generation
   b) Mod subculture
   c) Hippy movement
   d) Punk rock

The Tornados (Answers Page 198)

800. What was the name of The Tornados' first single?
   a) Telstar
   b) Robot
   c) Globetrotter
   d) Jungle Fever

801. Who was the lead singer of The Tornados?
   a) Clem Cattini
   b) George Bellamy
   c) Heinz Burt
   d) The Tornados were an instrumental group

802. What was the name of The Tornados' first album?
   a) Telstar
   b) The Tornados Play Telstar and Other Great Hits
   c) The Tornados Play the Exciting Sounds of the Ventures
   d) The Tornados Play the Hits of the Shadows

803. What was the name of The Tornados' drummer?
   a) Clem Cattini
   b) George Bellamy
   c) Heinz Burt
   d) Ray Elliott

Traffic (Answers Page 198)

804. Who was the lead singer of Traffic?
    a) Steve Winwood
    b) Jim Capaldi
    c) Dave Mason
    d) Chris Wood

805. What was the name of Traffic's first album?
    a) Mr. Fantasy
    b) Traffic
    c) John Barleycorn Must Die
    d) The Low Spark of High Heeled Boys

806. What was the name of Traffic's second album?
    a). Mr. Fantasy
    b) Traffic
    c) John Barleycorn Must Die
    d) The Low Spark of High Heeled Boys

807. Who played the drums for Traffic?
    a) Steve Winwood
    b) Jim Capaldi
    c) Dave Mason
    d) Chris Wood

808. What was the name of Traffic's third album?
    a). Mr. Fantasy
    b) Traffic
    c) John Barleycorn Must Die
    d) The Low Spark of High Heeled Boys

809. What was the name of Traffic's guitarist?
    a) Steve Winwood
    b) Jim Capaldi
    c) Dave Mason
    d) Chris Wood

Trapeze (Answers Page 198)

810. In what year was Trapeze formed as a band?
    a) 1966
    b) 1968
    c) 1970
    d) 1972

811. Who was the founding member and lead vocalist/bassist of Trapeze?
    a) Mel Galley
    b) Glenn Hughes
    c) Dave Holland
    d) Rob Kendrick

812. Trapeze is often associated with which musical genre?
    a) Progressive rock
    b) Psychedelic rock
    c) Jazz fusion
    d) Heavy metal

813. Which Trapeze album, released in 1970, featured the song "Medusa" and is considered one of their notable works?
    a) "You Are the Music... We're Just the Band"
    b) "Medusa"
    c) "Trapeze"
    d) "Hot Wire"

814. Prior to joining Deep Purple, Glenn Hughes, Trapeze's bassist and vocalist, briefly played with another famous guitarist. Who was this guitarist?
    a) Ritchie Blackmore
    b) Jimmy Page
    c) Eric Clapton
    d) Tony Iommi

Toe Fat (Answers)

792. a) David Byron and Ken Hensley
793. d) "Toe Fat"
794. c) Blues rock
795. b) "Toe Fat Two"

Tomorrow (Answers)

796. c) "My White Bicycle"
797. a) Steve Howe
798. b) 1967
799. b) Mod subculture

The Tornados (Answers)

800. d) Jungle Fever
801. d) The Tornados were an instrumental group
802. b) The Tornados Play Telstar and Other Great Hits
803. a) Clem Cattini

Traffic (Answers)

804. a) Steve Winwood
805. a) Mr. Fantasy
806. b) Traffic
807. b) Jim Capaldi
808. c) John Barleycorn Must Die
809. c) Dave Mason

Trapeze (Answers)

810. b) 1968
811. c) Dave Holland
812. c) Jazz fusion
813. a) "You Are the Music... We're Just the Band"
814. a) Ritchie Blackmore

The Tremeloes (Answers Page 204)

815. Who was the lead singer of The Tremeloes?
a) Brian Poole
b) Rick Westwood
c) Alan Blakley
d) Dave Munden

816. What was the name of The Tremeloes' first single?
a) Twist and Shout
b) Do You Love Me
c) Silence Is Golden
d). Here Comes My Baby

817. What was the name of The Tremeloes' first album?
a) Big Big Hits of '62
b) Twist and Shout
c) It's About Time
d) Brian Poole Is Here!

818. Who played the lead guitar for The Tremeloes?
a) Brian Poole
b) Rick Westwood
c) Alan Blakley
d) Dave Munden

819. What was the name of The Tremeloes' bassist?
a) Brian Poole
b) Rick Westwood
c) Alan Blakley
d) Chip Hawkes

T. Rex (Answers Page 204)

820. What was the real name of the lead singer and creative force
behind T. Rex?
a) Marc Bolan
b) Mick Jagger
c) David Bowie
d) Freddie Mercury

T. Rex (Answers Page 204)

821. T. Rex achieved significant commercial success with their 1971 album that featured hits like "Get It On" and "Hot Love." What is the title of this album?
a) "Electric Warrior"
b) "The Slider"
c) "Tanx"
d) "A Beard of Stars"

822. What was the original name of T. Rex when they first formed in the 1960s?
a) Tyrannosaurus Rex
b) The Electric Elves
c) The Cosmic Couriers
d) The Glam Rockers

823. T. Rex's iconic lead singer, Marc Bolan, was known for playing a distinctive guitar. What was the name of this unique guitar model?
a) Les Paul
b) Stratocaster
c) Flying V
d) Gibson SG

824. In 1972, T. Rex released an album that marked a departure from their glam rock sound, exploring a softer, more acoustic direction. What is the title of this album?
a) "Tanx"
b) "The Slider"
c) "Bolan Boogie"
d) "Zinc Alloy and the Hidden Riders of Tomorrow"

825. T. Rex's 1970 single "Ride a White Swan" is often considered the beginning of the glam rock era. Who played keyboards on this track and later became a successful solo artist?
a) Rick Wakeman
b) Elton John
c) Brian Eno
d) Tony Visconti

The Troggs (Answers Page 204)

826. What was the name of the Troggs' first hit single?
    a) "Wild Thing"
    b) "With a Girl Like You"
    c) "I Can't Control Myself"
    d) "Love Is All Around"

827. Which Troggs song topped the UK charts in July 1966?
    a) "Getaway"
    b) "Sunny Afternoon"
    c) "With a Girl Like You"
    d) "Bus Stop"

828. Who was the drummer of the Troggs?
    a) Ronnie Bond
    b) Pete Staples
    c) Reg Presley
    d) Chris Britton

829. Which Troggs song contains the lyrics "Your slacks are low and your hips are showin'"?
    a) "Reach Out I'll Be There"
    b) "I Can't Control Myself"
    c) "Stop Stop Stop"
    d) "No Milk Today"

830. Who replaced Ronnie Bond in the Troggs' lineup in 1969?
    a) Tony Murray
    b) Chris Britton
    c) Reg Presley
    d) Pete Staples

Tucky Buzzard (Answers Page 204)

831. Who was the lead singer of Tucky Buzzard?
    a) Jimmy Henderson
    b) Terry Taylor
    c) David Brown
    d) Nick Graham

Tucky Buzzard (Answers Page 204)

832. Tucky Buzzard's music is associated with which rock genre?
    a) Psychedelic rock
    b) Glam rock
    c) Progressive rock
    d) Hard rock

833. The band released their debut album in 1971. What was the title of this album?
    a) "Tucky Buzzard"
    b) "Warm Slash"
    c) "Coming on Again"
    d) "All Right on the Night"

834. Tucky Buzzard's lineup included members who previously played with which other well-known British rock band?
    a) The Rolling Stones
    b) Led Zeppelin
    c) The Yardbirds
    d) The Who

835. Which of the following songs is one of Tucky Buzzard's notable tracks?
    a) "Whole Lotta Love"
    b) "Sonic Love"
    c) "Space Oddity"
    d) "You Really Got Me"

The Undertakers (Answers Page 204)

836. What was the name of The Undertakers' lead vocalist?
    a) Jackie Lomax
    b) Tony Schofield
    c) Les Jones
    d) Mike Bennett

837. Which record label did The Undertakers sign with?
    a) Decca Records
    b) Pye Records
    c) Columbia Records

d) EMI Records
The Undertakers (Answers Page 204)

838. What was the name of The Undertakers' first single?
    a) "Just a Little Bit"
    b) "Money"
    c) "Unchain My Heart"
    d) "Everybody Loves A Lover"

839. What was the name of The Undertakers' bassist?
    a) Brian Jones
    b) Tony Schofield
    c) Les Jones
    d) Mike Bennett

840. What was the name of The Undertakers' lead guitarist?
    a) Brian Jones
    b) Tony Schofield
    c) Les Jones
    d) Mike Bennett

The Tremeloes (Answers)

815. d) Dave Munden
816. b) Do You Love Me
817. a) Big Big Hits of '62
818. b) Rick Westwood
819. d) Chip Hawkes

T. Rex (Answers)

820. a) Marc Bolan
821. a) "Electric Warrior"
822. a) Tyrannosaurus Rex
823. c) Flying V
824. d) "Zinc Alloy and the Hidden Riders of
    Tomorrow"
825. b) Elton John

The Troggs (Answers)

826. a) "Wild Thing"
827. c) "With a Girl Like You"
828. a) Ronnie Bond
829. b) "I Can't Control Myself"
830. a) Tony Murray

Tucky Buzzard (Answers)

831. a) Jimmy Henderson
832. d) Hard rock
833. b) "Warm Slash"
834. c) The Yardbirds
835.b) "Sonic Love"

The Undertakers (Answers)

836. a) Jackie Lomax
837. b) Pye Records
838. b) "Money"
839. c) Les Jones

840. b) Tony Schofield

Unit 4+2 (Answers Page 216)

841. What was the name of Unit 4+2's first hit single?
    a) "Concrete and Clay"
    b) "You've Got to Be Cruel to Be Kind"
    c) "I Will Return"
    d) "Green Fields"

842. Who was the lead singer of Unit 4+2?
    a) Brian Parker
    b) Tommy Moeller
    c) Russ Ballard
    d) Bob Henrit

843. Which Unit 4+2 song was covered by the Mamas & the Papas?
    a) "Concrete and Clay"
    b) "You've Got to Be Cruel to Be Kind"
    c) "I Will Return"
    d) "Green Fields"

844. Which member of Unit 4+2 co-wrote the song "God Gave Rock and Roll to You"?
    a) Brian Parker
    b) Tommy Moeller
    c) Russ Ballard
    d) Bob Henrit

845. Which Unit 4+2 song was covered by the Beach Boys?
    a) "Concrete and Clay"
    b) "You've Got to Be Cruel to Be Kind"
    c). "I Will Return"
    d) "Green Fields"

Uriah Heep (Answers Page 216)

846. What was the name of Uriah Heep's debut album?
    a) "Demons and Wizards"
    b) "Salisbury"
    c) "Very 'Eavy... Very 'Umble"
    d) "Look at Yourself"

Uriah Heep (Answers Page 216)

847. Who was the lead vocalist of Uriah Heep from 1976 to 1986?
a) David Byron
b) John Lawton
c) Bernie Shaw
d) Peter Goalby

848. Which Uriah Heep song was covered by Blackfoot in 1983?
a) "Easy Livin'"
b) "Gypsy"
c) "Stealin'"
d) "July Morning"

849. Who played bass guitar on Uriah Heep's 1972 album "Demons and Wizards"?
a) Gary Thain
b) John Wetton
c) Trevor Bolder
d) Mark Clarke

850. Which Uriah Heep song contains the lyrics "I'm just a simple man, trying to make my way in the night"?
a) "The Wizard"
b) "Sunrise"
c) "Rainbow Demon"
d) "Sweet Lorraine"

851. Which Uriah Heep album features the song "Lady in Black"?
a) "Look at Yourself"
b) "Demons and Wizards"
c) "The Magician's Birthday"
d) "Sweet Freedom"

852. Who played drums on Uriah Heep's 1971 album "Salisbury"?
a) Keith Baker
b) Nigel Olsson
c) Lee Kerslake

d) Ian Paice

Van Morrison (Answers Page 216)

853. What was the name of Van Morrison's first solo album?
a) "Astral Weeks"
b) "Moondance"
c) "Blowin' Your Mind!"
d) "Tupelo Honey"

854. Which Van Morrison song was covered by Them, the band he fronted in the 1960s?
a) "Brown Eyed Girl"
b) "Gloria"
c) "Into the Mystic"
d) "Domino"

855. Which Van Morrison song contains the lyrics "It's too late to stop now"?
a) "And It Stoned Me"
b) "Caravan"
c) "Wild Night"
d) "Jackie Wilson Said (I'm in Heaven When You Smile)"

856. Who played guitar on Van Morrison's 1967 album "Blowin' Your Mind!"?
a) Eric Clapton
b) Jimmy Page
c) Peter Green
d) Rory Gallagher

857. Which Van Morrison song was used in the 1994 film "Reality Bites"?
a) "Brown Eyed Girl"
b) "Moondance"
c) "Wild Night"
d) "Tupelo Honey"

858. Which Van Morrison album features the song "Madame George"?
a) "Astral Weeks"
b) "Moondance"
c) "His Band and the Street Choir"

d) "Tupelo Honey"

Van Morrison (Answers Page 216)

859. Who played drums on Van Morrison's 1970 album "Moondance"?
a) Jim Keltner
b) Levon Helm
c) Ringo Starr
d) Charlie Watts

860. Which Van Morrison album features the song "And It Stoned Me"?
a) "Astral Weeks"
b) "Moondance"
c) "His Band and the Street Choir"
d) "Tupelo Honey"

861. Who played bass guitar on Van Morrison's 1968 album "Astral Weeks"?
a) Jack Bruce
b) John Paul Jones
c) Paul McCartney
d) Noel Redding

The Who (Answers Page 216 & 217)

862. Who was the lead guitarist of The Who?
a) Pete Townshend
b) Roger Daltrey
c) John Entwistle
d) Keith Moon

863. What was the title of The Who's debut album released in 1965?
a) My Generation
b) Quadrophenia
c) Tommy
d) A Quick One

The Who (Answers Page 216 & 217)

864. Which song by The Who features the iconic lyric "Hope I die before I get old"?
a) My Generation
b) Pinball Wizard
c) Substitute
d) I Can't Explain

865. What instrument did John Entwistle play in The Who?
a) Guitar
b) Drums
c) Bass
d) Keyboards

866. Who was The Who's original drummer?
a) Keith Moon
b) Ringo Starr
c) Charlie Watts
d) Kenny Jones

867. Which rock opera by The Who tells the story of a "deaf, dumb, and blind" boy?
a) Tommy
b) Quadrophenia
c) Who's Next
d) A Quick One

868. Which member of The Who wrote the majority of the band's songs?
a) Roger Daltrey
b) Keith Moon
c) Pete Townshend
d) John Entwistle

869. What was The Who's first UK Top 10 single?
a) I Can't Explain
b) Substitute
c) Happy Jack
d) Pictures of Lily

The Who (Answers Page 216 & 217)

870. Who replaced Keith Moon as The Who's drummer after his death?
a) Kenny Jones
b) Zak Starkey
c) Simon Phillips
d) Alan White

871. What was the title of The Who's second studio album released in 1966?
a) A Quick One
b) My Generation
c) The Who Sell Out
d) Face Dances

872. In which year did The Who perform at the Woodstock Festival?
a) 1967
b) 1969
c) 1971
d) 1973

873. Which song by The Who is known for its iconic windmill guitar playing by Pete Townshend?
a) Baba O'Riley
b) Pinball Wizard
c) I Can See for Miles
d) Magic Bus

874. Which album by The Who includes the hit single "Behind Blue Eyes"?
a) Who's Next
b) Quadrophenia
c) The Who by Numbers
d) Tommy

875. Who was The Who's lead vocalist?
a) Keith Moon
b) John Entwistle
c) Roger Daltrey

d) Pete Townshend

The Who (Answers Page 216 & 217)

876. What was The Who's final studio album with their original lineup?
a) Who Are You
b) It's Hard
c) Quadrophenia
d) Endless Wire

877. In which year were The Who inducted into the Rock and Roll Hall of Fame?
a) 1989
b) 1992
c) 1998
d) 2001

The Wilde Flowers (Answers Page 217)

878. Who was the lead vocalist of Wilde Flowers?
a). Kevin Ayers
b) Brian Hopper
c) Richard Sinclair
d) Robert Wyatt

879. Who was the lead guitarist and co-lead vocalist of Wilde Flowers?
a) Kevin Ayers
b) Brian Hopper
c) Richard Sinclair
d) Robert Wyatt

880. Which member of Wilde Flowers went on to join the founding lineup of Soft Machine?
a) Kevin Ayers
b) Brian Hopper
c) Richard Sinclair
d) Robert Wyatt

The Wilde Flowers (Answers Page 217)

881. What was the primary musical style of the Wilde Flowers?
    a) Psychedelic Rock
    b) Blues
    c) Progressive Rock
    d) Folk

882. In which year did the Wilde Flowers disband?
    a) 1965
    b) 1967
    c) 1969
    d) 1971

883. What was the Wilde Flowers' debut single?
    a) "Memories"
    b) "Parchman Farm"
    c) "Impotence"
    d) "She Loves to Hurt"

884. What was the title of the Wilde Flowers' only studio album released in 1969?
    a) "Brewed in Canterbury"
    b) "A Retrospective"
    c) "The Wilde Flowers Chronicles"
    d) They did not release a studio album

The Wimple Winch (Answers Page 217)

885. Who was the lead vocalist of Wimple Winch?
    a) James Wynne
    b) Johnny Carroll
    c) Barry Reynolds
    d) Terry McKay

886. What was the title of Wimple Winch's debut single released in 1966?
    a) "Save My Soul"
    b) "Marmalade Hair"
    c) "Rumble on Mersey Square South"
    d) "Atmospheres of My Mind"

The Wimple Winch (Answers Page 217)

887. Who wrote the majority of Wimple Winch's original songs?
   a) Barry Reynolds
   b) James Wynne
   c) Johnny Carroll
   d) Terry McKay

888. What instrument did Johnny Carroll play in Wimple Winch?
   a) Guitar
   b) Drums
   c) Bass
   d) Keyboards

889. What was the title of Wimple Winch's B-side to the single "Save My Soul"?
   a) "Marmalade Hair"
   b) "Rumble on Mersey Square South"
   c) "Atmospheres of My Mind"
   d) "The Best of Faces"

890. Who produced Wimple Winch's singles and recordings?
   a) Joe Meek
   b) George Martin
   c) Shel Talmy
   d) Jimmy Page

891. What was the title of Wimple Winch's follow-up single to "Save My Soul"?
   a) "Marmalade Hair"
   b) "Rumble on Mersey Square South"
   c) "Atmospheres of My Mind"
   d) "Lollipop Minds"

892. Which member of Wimple Winch later joined the band Cochise?
   a) Barry Reynolds
   b) James Wynne
   c) Johnny Carroll
   d) Terry McKay

Wishbone Ash (Answers Page 217)

893. In which year was Wishbone Ash formed?
    a) 1967
    b) 1969
    c) 1971
    d) 1973

894. What is the signature sound of Wishbone Ash known for?
    a) Heavy Metal
    b) Progressive Rock
    c) Blues Rock
    d) Jazz Fusion

895. Who is the founding member and lead guitarist of Wishbone Ash?
    a) Martin Turner
    b) Ted Turner
    c) Andy Powell
    d) Steve Upton

896. What was the title of Wishbone Ash's debut album released in 1970?
    a) "Wishbone Ash"
    b) "Pilgrimage"
    c) "Argus"
    d) "Wishbone Four"

897. Which Wishbone Ash album is often considered their masterpiece and a classic of the progressive rock genre?
    a) "Wishbone Ash"
    b) "Argus"
    c) "Pilgrimage"
    d) "New England"

898. What song by Wishbone Ash features a distinctive opening harmony guitar riff?
    a) "Blowin' Free"
    b) "The King Will Come"
    c) "Argus"
    d) "Throw Down the Sword"

Wishbone Ash (Answers Page 217)

899. Which album marked the departure of Ted Turner and the introduction of Laurie Wisefield as the second guitarist for Wishbone Ash?
a) "Wishbone Ash"
b) "Argus"
c) "There's the Rub"
d) "Just Testing"

900. Which drummer was part of the original Wishbone Ash lineup?
a) Steve Upton
b) Rob Townsend
c) Ray Weston
d) Joe Crabtree

901. What was the title of Wishbone Ash's first live album released in 1973?
a) "Live Dates"
b) "Live Dates 2"
c) "Live in Tokyo"
d) "Live at the Marquee"

902. What is the title of the 1976 studio album by Wishbone Ash that includes the song "The King Will Come"?
a) "Locked In"
b) "Front Page News"
c) "New England"
d) "Blue Horizon"

Unit 4+2 (Answers)

841. d) "Green Fields"
842. b) Tommy Moeller
843. a) "Concrete and Clay"
844. c) Russ Ballard
845. d) "Green Fields"

Uriah Heep (Answers)

846. c) "Very 'Eavy… Very 'Umble"
847. b) John Lawton
848. b) "Gypsy"
849. a) Gary Thain
850. b) "Sunrise"
851. c) "The Magician's Birthday"
852. a) Keith Baker

Van Morrison (Answers)

853. c) "Blowin' Your Mind!"
854. b) "Gloria"
855. b) "Caravan"
856. b) Jimmy Page
857. c) "Wild Night"
858. a) "Astral Weeks"
859. a) Jim Keltner
860. b) "Moondance"
861. a) Jack Bruce

The Who (Answers)

862. a) Pete Townshend
863. a) My Generation
864. a) My Generation
865. c) Bass
866. a) Keith Moon
867. a) Tommy
868. c) Pete Townshend
869. a) I Can't Explain
870. a) Kenny Jones
871. a) A Quick One

The Who (Answers)

872. b) 1969
873. a) Baba O'Riley
874. a) Who's Next
875. c) Roger Daltrey
876. b) It's Hard
877. a) 1989

The Wilde Flowers (Answers)

878. a). Kevin Ayers
879. b) Brian Hopper
880. d) Robert Wyatt
881. a) Psychedelic Rock
882. b) 1967
883. c) "Impotence"
884. d) They did not release a studio album

The Wimple Winch (Answers)

885. c) Barry Reynolds
886. a) "Save My Soul"
887. b) James Wynne
888. a) Guitar
889. c) "Atmospheres of My Mind"
890. a) Joe Meek
891. b) "Rumble on Mersey Square South"
892. a) Barry Reynolds

Wishbone Ash (Answers)

893. b) 1969
894. c) Blues Rock
895. c) Andy Powell
896. a) "Wishbone Ash"
897. b) "Argus"
898. a) "Blowin' Free"
899. c) "There's the Rub"
900. a) Steve Upton
901. a) "Live Dates"
902. b) "Front Page News"

The Yardbirds (Answers Page 223)

903. What year was The Yardbirds formed?
    a) 1955
    b) 1962
    c) 1965
    d) 1968

904. Who was The Yardbirds' original lead guitarist?
    a) Eric Clapton
    b) Jimmy Page
    c) Jeff Beck
    d) Keith Relf

905. Which Yardbirds hit song features a distinctive harmonica riff?
    a) "Heart Full of Soul"
    b) "For Your Love"
    c) "Shapes of Things"
    d) "Over Under Sideways Down"

906. What instrument did Jeff Beck play in The Yardbirds?
    a) Guitar
    b) Bass
    c) Drums
    d) Keyboards

907. Who replaced Paul Samwell-Smith as The Yardbirds' bassist?
    a) Chris Dreja
    b) Jimmy Page
    c) Jeff Beck
    d) John Paul Jones

908. What was the title of The Yardbirds' first album?
    a) "Five Live Yardbirds"
    b) "Having a Rave Up"
    c) "Roger the Engineer"
    d) "Little Games"

The Yardbirds (Answers Page 223)

909. Which Yardbirds song features the famous line "I wish you
   would"?
   a) "Happenings Ten Years Time Ago"
   b) "Over Under Sideways Down"
   c) "Shapes of Things"
   d) "I'm a Man"

910. Who was The Yardbirds' lead vocalist?
   a) Keith Relf
   b) Eric Clapton
   c) Jeff Beck
   d) Jimmy Page

911. What was the last studio album released by The Yardbirds in
   the 1960s?
   a) "Five Live Yardbirds"
   b) "Little Games"
   c) "For Your Love"
   d) "Roger the Engineer"

912. Which Yardbirds song includes the lyric "You're a better
   man than I"?
   a) "For Your Love"
   b) "Heart Full of Soul"
   c) "I'm a Man"
   d) "Shapes of Things"

913. Who played the bass guitar on The Yardbirds' hit song "For
   Your Love"?
   a) Paul Samwell-Smith
   b) Chris Dreja
   c) Jimmy Page
   d) Jeff Beck

914. What was the original title of "Heart Full of Soul" before it
   was changed?
   a) "Raga Muffin"
   b) "Evil Hearted You"
   c) "New York City Blues"

d) "Stroll On"

The Yardbirds (Answers Page 223)

915. In which year did Jeff Beck leave The Yardbirds?
    a) 1965
    b) 1966
    c) 1967
    d) 1968

916. What was the final lineup of The Yardbirds in the 1960s?
    a) Clapton, Page, Dreja, McCarty
    b) Beck, Page, Dreja, McCarty
    c) Relf, Page, Dreja, McCarty
    d) Clapton, Beck, Dreja, McCarty

917. What was The Yardbirds' last single released in the 1960s?
    a) "Dazed and Confused"
    b) "Goodnight Sweet Josephine"
    c) "Ha Ha Said the Clown"
    d) "Think About It"

Yes (Answers Page 223)

918. When was the progressive rock band Yes formed?
    a) 1965
    b) 1968
    c) 1971
    d) 1974

919. Who was the original lead vocalist of Yes?
    a) Jon Anderson
    b) Chris Squire
    c) Rick Wakeman
    d) Steve Howe

920. Which Yes album is known for its cover featuring a floating self-titled logo?
    a) "Close to the Edge"
    b) "Fragile"
    c) "Tales from Topographic Oceans"
    d) "Relayer"

Yes (Answers Page 223)

921. Who replaced Bill Bruford as Yes' drummer in the early 1970s?
a) Carl Palmer
b) Alan White
c) Bill Ward
d) Phil Collins

922. What instrument did Chris Squire play in Yes?
a) Guitar
b) Bass
c) Keyboards
d) Drums

923. Which Yes song features the lyrics "I've seen all good people turn their heads each day so satisfied I'm on my way"?
a) "Roundabout"
b) "Owner of a Lonely Heart"
c) "Heart of the Sunrise"
d) "Long Distance Runaround"

924. Who joined Yes as the keyboardist for the album "Fragile"?
a) Rick Wakeman
b) Tony Kaye
c) Patrick Moraz
d) Geoff Downes

925. What is the title of Yes' breakthrough album released in 1971?
a) "Fragile"
b) "The Yes Album"
c) "Close to the Edge"
d) "Going for the One"

926. Who was the guitarist known for his intricate playing style in Yes?
a) Steve Howe
b) Trevor Rabin
c) Peter Banks
d) Billy Sherwood

Yes (Answers Page 223)

927. In what year did Yes release the album "Tales from Topographic Oceans"?
a) 1972
b) 1973
c) 1974
d) 1975

928. Who was the original drummer for Yes?
a) Bill Bruford
b) Alan White
c) Tony Kaye
d) Chris Squire

929. What is the title of the album that features Yes' hit single "Owner of a Lonely Heart"?
a) "90125"
b) "Drama"
c) "Big Generator"
d) "Tormato"

930. Which Yes album was their first to feature Trevor Horn on vocals?
a) "Going for the One"
b) "Drama"
c) "Tormato"
d) "90125"

931. What is the name of the live album released by Yes in 1973?
a) "Yessongs"
b) "Keys to Ascension"
c) "Union"
d) "Symphonic Live"

932. Who replaced Jon Anderson as the lead vocalist for a brief period in the late 1970s?
a) Trevor Rabin
b) Jon Davison
c) Benoît David
d) Geoff Downes

The Yardbirds (Answers)

903. b) 1962
904. a) Eric Clapton
905. a) "Heart Full of Soul"
906. a) Guitar
907. a) Chris Dreja
908. a) "Five Live Yardbirds"
909. b) "Over Under Sideways Down"
910. a) Keith Relf
911. b) "Little Games"
912. c) "I'm a Man"
913. a) Paul Samwell-Smith
914. a) "Raga Muffin"
915. b) 1966
916. b) Beck, Page, Dreja, McCarty
917. c) "Ha Ha Said the Clown"

Yes (Answers)

918. b) 1968
919. a) Jon Anderson
920. b) "Fragile"
921. b) Alan White
922. b) Bass
923. d) "Long Distance Runaround"
924. a) Rick Wakeman
925. b) "The Yes Album"
926. a) Steve Howe
927. b) 1973
928. a) Bill Bruford
929. a) "90125"
930. b) "Drama"
931. a) "Yessongs"
932. c) Benoît David

The Zombies (Answers Page 227)

933. What year was The Zombies formed?
    a) 1962
    b) 1964
    c) 1966
    d) 1968

934. Who was The Zombies' lead vocalist and primary
    songwriter?
    a) Rod Argent
    b) Colin Blunstone
    c) Chris White
    d) Hugh Grundy

935. What was The Zombies' debut studio album released in
    1965?
    a) "Odessey and Oracle"
    b) "Begin Here"
    c) "The Zombies"
    d) "Still Got That Hunger"

936. Which hit single by The Zombies reached number 2 on the
    US Billboard Hot 100 in 1964?
    a) "She's Not There"
    b) "Tell Her No"
    c) "Time of the Season"
    d) "Care of Cell 44"

937. What instrument did Rod Argent play in The Zombies?
    a) Guitar
    b) Bass
    c) Keyboards
    d) Drums

938. What was the title of The Zombies' second studio album
    released in 1965?
    a) "Odessey and Oracle"
    b) "The Zombies"
    c) "Still Got That Hunger"
    d) "I Love You"

The Zombies (Answers Page 227)

939. Which song from the album "Odessey and Oracle" became a major hit after its release?
a) "Time of the Season"
b) "Tell Her No"
c) "Care of Cell 44"
d) "A Rose for Emily"

940. Who wrote most of The Zombies' original songs?
a) Rod Argent
b) Colin Blunstone
c) Chris White
d) Hugh Grundy

941. What was the last track on the album "Odessey and Oracle"?
a) "Care of Cell 44"
b) "This Will Be Our Year"
c) "Time of the Season"
d) "Butcher's Tale (Western Front 1914)"

942. In what year did The Zombies disband initially?
a) 1967
b) 1969
c) 1971
d) 1973

943. What was the name of The Zombies' original bassist?
a) Chris White
b) Paul Atkinson
c) Hugh Grundy
d) Jim Rodford

944. What instrument did Paul Atkinson play in The Zombies?
a) Guitar
b) Bass
c) Keyboards
d) Drums

The Zombies (Answers Page 227)

945. Which member of The Zombies became a successful solo
artist in the 1970s?
a) Colin Blunstone
b) Rod Argent
c) Chris White
d) Hugh Grundy

946. Who produced The Zombies' hit single "Time of the
Season"?
a) George Martin
b) Brian Wilson
c) Paul McCartney
d) Chris White

947. In which city did The Zombies record most of their
material?
a) London
b) Liverpool
c) Los Angeles
d) New York

948. What was The Zombies' final studio album before their
initial disbandment in the late 1960s?
a) "Odessey and Oracle"
b) "R.I.P."
c) "New World"
d) "Still Got That Hunger"

The Zombies (Answers)

933. a) 1962
934. b) Colin Blunstone
935. b) "Begin Here"
936. a) "She's Not There"
937. c) Keyboards
938. b) "The Zombies"
939. a) "Time of the Season"
940. a) Rod Argent
941. d) "Butcher's Tale (Western Front 1914)"
942. b) 1969
943. a) Chris White
944. a) Guitar
945. a) Colin Blunstone
946. b) Brian Wilson
947. c) Los Angeles
948. b) "R.I.P.

British Rock Musicians Of The 1960s

Ginger Baker: (Answers Page 239)

949. What is Ginger Baker's full name?
    a) Peter Edward Baker
    b) John Henry Baker
    c) Anthony Charles Baker
    d) Peter Edward Ginger Baker

950. Ginger Baker was a renowned drummer and a member of which influential British rock band in the 1960s?
    a) The Rolling Stones
    b) Cream
    c) The Who
    d) The Yardbirds

951. In addition to drums, Ginger Baker played which other percussion instrument, contributing to his distinctive drumming style?
    a) Congas
    b) Bongos
    c) Timbales
    d) Marimba

952. What is the title of Ginger Baker's debut solo album, released in 1970?
    a) "Ginger Baker's Air Force"
    b) "Stratavarious"
    c) "Mad Jack"
    d) "Horses & Trees"

Jeff Beck: (Answers Page 239)

953. Which Jeff Beck album features the instrumental hit "Cause We've Ended as Lovers"?
a) "Truth"
b) "Blow by Blow"
c) "Wired"
d) "Beck-Ola"

954. Which technique is Jeff Beck known for popularizing on the guitar, involving rapid picking with the fingers?
a) Tapping
b) Vibrato
c) Slapping
d) Fingerstyle picking

955. What was the title of Jeff Beck's first solo album released in 1968?
a) "Truth"
b) "Beck-Ola"
c) "Blow by Blow"
d) "Jeff Beck Group"

Ritchie Blackmore: (Answers Page 239)

956. What is Ritchie Blackmore's full name?
a) Richard James Blackmore
b) Richard Hugh Blackmore
c) Richard John Blackmore
d) Richard David Blackmore

957. What is the title of the instrumental guitar piece often associated with Ritchie Blackmore, released by Deep Purple in 1972?
a) "Smoke on the Water"
b) "Highway Star"
c) "Lazy"
d) "Wring That Neck"

Ritchie Blackmore: (Answers Page 239)

958. In which year did Ritchie Blackmore leave Deep Purple to
form Rainbow?
a) 1972
b) 1975
c) 1978
d) 1980

Bill Bruford: (Answers Page 239)

959. What is Bill Bruford's full name?
a) William John Bruford
b) Benjamin Richard Bruford
c) Brian Michael Bruford
d) Bradley Christopher Bruford
(a) William John Bruford

960. Bill Bruford is a renowned drummer who gained fame as a
member of which progressive rock band in the 1970s?
a) Yes
b) Genesis
c) King Crimson
d) Emerson, Lake & Palmer (ELP)

961. What is the title of the instrumental track often associated
with Bill Bruford, released on the King Crimson album
"Red"?
a) "Larks' Tongues in Aspic"
b) "Starless"
c) "One More Red Nightmare"
d) "Red"

962. Bill Bruford was a founding member of which progressive
rock band before joining King Crimson?
a) Yes
b) Genesis
c) Jethro Tull
d) Emerson, Lake & Palmer (ELP)

Eric Burdon: (Answers Page 239)

963. What is Eric Burdon's full name?
   a) Eric Victor Burdon
   b) Eric Patrick Burdon
   c) Eric John Burdon
   d) Eric Michael Burdon

964. Eric Burdon gained fame as the lead vocalist of which influential British rock band in the 1960s?
   a) The Rolling Stones
   b) The Animals
   c) The Yardbirds
   d) The Who

965. In addition to singing, Eric Burdon is known for playing which musical instrument?
   a) Guitar
   b) Harmonica
   c) Keyboards
   d) Bass

966. What' the title of Eric Burdon's debut solo album, released in 1966?
   a) "Winds of Change"
   b) "Eric Is Here"
   c) "The Twain Shall Meet"
   d) "House of the Rising Sun"

Jim Capaldi: (Answers Page 239)

967. What is Jim Capaldi's full name?
   a) James Robert Capaldi
   b) James George Capaldi
   c) James Nicholas Capaldi
   d) James Anthony Capaldi

Jim Capaldi: (Answers Page 239)

968. Jim Capaldi was a founding member and drummer of which British rock band?
a) The Rolling Stones
b) Traffic
c) Cream
d) The Who

969. In addition to drumming, Jim Capaldi was known for his skills in which musical instrument?
a) Guitar
b) Bass
c) Keyboards
d) Harmonica

Eric Clapton: (Answers Page 240)

970. Eric Clapton co-founded the supergroup Cream with which other musicians?
a) Jack Bruce and Ginger Baker
b) Jimmy Page and John Bonham
c) Jeff Beck and Keith Moon
d) George Harrison and Ringo Starr

971. Which Eric Clapton song is a tribute to his son, Conor, who tragically passed away?
a) "Layla"
b) "Tears in Heaven"
c) "Wonderful Tonight"
d) "Cocaine"

972. Eric Clapton has been inducted into the Rock and Roll Hall of Fame three times. Which bands is he associated with in these inductions?
a) Cream, The Yardbirds, Blind Faith
b) Cream, The Yardbirds, Derek and the Dominos
c) Cream, The Rolling Stones, Blind Faith
d) The Yardbirds, Cream, The Beatles

Roger Daltrey: (Answers Page 240)

973. What is Roger Daltrey's full name?
   a) Roger Harry Daltrey
   b) Roger Keith Daltrey
   c) Roger James Daltrey
   d) Roger David Daltrey

974. In addition to singing, what instrument does Roger Daltrey play?
   a) Guitar
   b) Bass
   c) Drums
   d) Harmonica

975. What was the title of Roger Daltrey's debut solo album released in 1973?
   a) "One of the Boys"
   b) "Ride a Rock Horse"
   c) "McVicar"
   d) "Daltrey"

Keith Emerson: (Answers Page 240)

976. What was Keith Emerson's full name?
   a) Keith Richard Emerson
   b) Keith Noel Emerson
   c) Keith James Emerson
   d) Keith Elton Emerson

977. What was the title of Keith Emerson's only solo studio album released in 1980?
   a) "Keith Emerson Band"
   b) "Honky"
   c) "At the Movies"
   d) "Nighthawks"

Keith Emerson: (Answers Page 240)

978. What innovative keyboard instrument did Keith Emerson popularize in rock music during the 1970s?
a) Mellotron
b) Moog synthesizer
c) Hammond organ
d) Clavinet

979. In 1971, Keith Emerson composed a rock adaptation of which classical work, featuring in ELP's album "Pictures at an Exhibition"?
a) "The Planets" by Gustav Holst
b) "Rhapsody in Blue" by George Gershwin
c) "Pictures at an Exhibition" by Modest Mussorgsky
d) "The Nutcracker Suite" by Pyotr Ilyich Tchaikovsky

Mick Jagger: (Answers Page 240)

980. What is Mick Jagger's full name?
a) Michael Philip Jagger
b) Mick James Jagger
c) Mark Peter Jagger
d) Martin Paul Jagger

981. What is the title of Mick Jagger's first solo album, released in 1985?
a) "She's the Boss"
b) "Primitive Cool"
c) "Wandering Spirit"
d) "Goddess in the Doorway"

982. In addition to singing, Mick Jagger is known for playing which instrument in The Rolling Stones?
a) Guitar
b) Bass
c) Harmonica
d) Keyboards

Jimmy Page: (Answers Page 240)

983. What is Jimmy Page's full name?
   a) James Patrick Page
   b) James Douglas Page
   c) James Robert Page
   d) James William Page

984. Which iconic double-necked guitar did Jimmy Page
   famously use during Led Zeppelin performances?
   a) Gibson Les Paul
   b) Fender Stratocaster
   c) Rickenbacker 12-string
   d) Gibson EDS-1275

985. In addition to being a guitarist, Jimmy Page co-produced
   many Led Zeppelin albums. Which pseudonym did he use
   for his production credits?
   a) Firebird
   b) Zoso
   c) The Hermit
   d) Brown Bomber

986. Jimmy Page is known for his exceptional skills not only as a
   guitarist but also as a:
   a) Drummer
   b) Bassist
   c) Keyboardist
   d) Singer

Robert Plant: (Answers Page 240)

987. What is Robert Plant's full name?
   a) Robert Anthony Plant
   b) Robert John Plant
   c) Robert William Plant
   d) Robert Michael Plant

988. What is the title of Robert Plant's debut solo album released in 1982?
   a) "Shaken 'n' Stirred"
   b) "Now and Zen"
   c) "Pictures at Eleven"
   d) "The Principle of Moments"

989. Which Led Zeppelin song features Robert Plant's iconic vocal performance and lyrics inspired by J.R.R. Tolkien's "The Lord of the Rings"?
   a) "Whole Lotta Love"
   b) "Kashmir"
   c) "The Battle Of Evermore"
   d) "Black Dog"

Rick Wakeman: (Answers Page 241)

990. What is Rick Wakeman's full name?
   a) Richard Christopher Wakeman
   b) Robert Edward Wakeman
   c) Raymond William Wakeman
   d) Ronald Paul Wakeman

991. Rick Wakeman is best known as a virtuoso keyboardist and was a member of which legendary progressive rock band?
   a) Genesis
   b) Yes
   c) Pink Floyd
   d) King Crimson

Rick Wakeman: (Answers Page 241)

992. In addition to keyboards, Rick Wakeman is skilled at playing which other instrument, often incorporating it into his performances?
a) Guitar
b) Violin
c) Flute
d) Keytar

993. What is the title of Rick Wakeman's concept album released in 1973 that is based on a famous work of literature?
a) "Journey to the Centre of the Earth"
b) "The Myths and Legends of King Arthur and the Knights of the Round Table"
c) "The Six Wives of Henry VIII"
d) "The Hound of the Baskervilles"

Roger Waters: (Answers Page 241)

994. What is Roger Waters' full name?
a) Roger David Waters
b) Roger George Waters
c) Roger Charles Waters
d) Roger James Waters

995. Which instrument did Roger Waters primarily play in Pink Floyd?
a) Guitar
b) Drums
c) Bass
d) Keyboards

996. What is the title of the Pink Floyd album for which Roger Waters wrote the majority of the lyrics but had left the band by its release?
a) "Meddle"
b) "Animals"
c) "The Final Cut"
d) "Atom Heart Mother"

Roger Waters: (Answers Page 241)

997. What was the title of Roger Waters' debut solo album
released in 1984?
a) "Amused to Death"
b) "The Pros and Cons of Hitch Hiking"
c) "Is This the Life We Really Want?"
d) "Radio K.A.O.S."

Steve Winwood: (Answers Page 241)

998. What is Steve Winwood's full name?
a) Stephen Andrew Winwood
b) Stephen Lawrence Winwood
c) Stephen Thomas Winwood
d) Stephen Lawrence Davis

999. Steve Winwood gained fame as a member of which
influential British rock band in the 1960s?
a) The Rolling Stones
b) The Who
c) Cream
d) Traffic

1000.	In 2004, Steve Winwood was inducted into the
Rock and Roll Hall of Fame as a member of which band?
a) Cream
b) The Spencer Davis Group
c) Blind Faith
d) Traffic

Ginger Baker (Answers)

949. a) Peter Edward Baker
950. b) Cream
951. a) Congas
952. b) "Stratavarious"

Jeff Beck (Answers)

953. b) "Blow by Blow"
954. d) Fingerstyle picking
955. a) "Truth"

Ritchie Blackmore (Answers)

956. b) Richard Hugh Blackmore
957. d) "Wring That Neck"
958. b) 1975

Bill Bruford (Answers)

959. a) William John Bruford
960. c) King Crimson
961. a) "Larks' Tongues in Aspic"
962. a) Yes

Eric Burdon (Answers)

963. a) Eric Victor Burdon
964. b) The Animals
965. b) Harmonica
966. a) "Winds of Change"

Jim Capaldi (Answers)

967. a) James Robert Capaldi
968. b) Traffic
969. c) Keyboards

Eric Clapton (Answers)

970. a) Jack Bruce and Ginger Baker
971. b) "Tears in Heaven"
972. b) Cream, The Yardbirds, Derek and the Dominos

Roger Daltrey (Answers)

973. b) Roger Keith Daltrey
974. d) Harmonica
975. d) "Daltrey"

Keith Emerson (Answers)

976. c) Keith James Emerson
977. d) "Honky"
978. b) Moog synthesizer
979. c) "Pictures at an Exhibition" by Modest
     Mussorgsky

Mick Jagger (Answers)

980. a) Michael Philip Jagger
981. a) "She's the Boss"
982. c) Harmonica

Jimmy Page (Answers)

983. a) James Patrick Page
984. d) Gibson EDS-1275
985. c) The Hermit
986. c) Keyboardist

Robert Plant (Answers)

987. b) Robert Anthony Plant
988. c) "Pictures at Eleven"
989. c) "The Battle Of Evermore"

Rick Wakeman (Answers)

990. a) Richard Christopher Wakeman
991. b) Yes
992. c) Keytar
993. b) "The Myths and Legends of King Arthur and the
     Knights of the Round Table"

Roger Waters (Answers)

994. a) Roger David Waters
995. c) Bass
996. c) "The Final Cut"
997. b) "The Pros and Cons of Hitch Hiking"

Steve Winwood (Answers)

998. c) Stephen Thomas Winwood
999. d) Traffic
1000.   b) The Spencer Davis Group